CAPTIVE TO THE WORD OF GOD

Captive to the Word of God

Engaging the Scriptures for
Contemporary Theological Reflection

⸺⟨∞∞⟩⸺

Miroslav Volf

WILLIAM B. EERDMANS PUBLISHING COMPANY
GRAND RAPIDS, MICHIGAN / CAMBRIDGE, U.K.

Published 2010 by

Wm. B. Eerdmans Publishing Co.

2140 Oak Industrial Drive N.E., Grand Rapids, Michigan 49505 /

P.O. Box 163, Cambridge CB3 9PU U.K.

Printed in the United States of America

15 14 13 12 11   7 6 5 4 3 2

Library of Congress Cataloging-in-Publication Data

Volf, Miroslav.

Captive to the word of God: engaging the scriptures
for contemporary theological reflection / Miroslav Volf.

p.   cm.

ISBN 978-0-8028-6590-8 (pbk.: alk. paper)

1. Bible — Criticism, interpretation, etc.   I. Title.

BS511.3.V65   2010

220.6 — dc22

2010044315

www.eerdmans.com

To the Meyes

Contents

———❧———

CONTENTS

PART I

Doing Theology

CHAPTER ONE

Reading the Bible Theologically

Introduction

In this book I, a systematic theologian, interpret texts of the Christian Scriptures. This may be all that you, the reader, want and need to know by way of introduction. If so, you may proceed to the subsequent chapters. For those who want more introduction, however, I discuss in this opening chapter why the interpretation of Scripture is important for theologians and what I as a theologian bring to the reading of Scripture. I do not, strictly speaking, argue my positions, but neither do I simply state them. Instead, I offer what might be called reasoned explications of my views.

As will be manifest to anyone who peruses the pages of this book, I am doing neither exegesis in the manner of a modern biblical scholar, nor devotional reading in the manner of a lay Christian, to name just two prevalent approaches to interpreting the Bible. Each of these ways of en-

I am grateful to my Yale colleagues John Collins, Jeremy Hultin, Dale Martin, Adela Yarbro Collins, and Tom Troeger, as well as to Timothy George and Marianne Meye Thompson for reading drafts of this chapter and discussing it with me. So did the circle of doctoral students at Yale (Matthew Croasmun, Terry J. Dumansky, Marcus Elder, Layne Jacobs, Natalia Marandiuc, Luke Morehead, Stephen Ogden, Devin Singh, Erinn Staley, and Linn Tonstad). To all of them I am deeply grateful.

gaging the Bible is internally diverse; and at least among the biblical scholars, the parameters of appropriate biblical interpretation continue to be debated.[1] However, both approaches are different from what I do here, even if the demarcation lines are not easy to draw because devotional habits of the heart and exegetical habits of the mind are both essential dimensions of the more integrated approach that I take here. Properly speaking, the essays in this book are *theological readings* of biblical texts.

What do I mean by "theological readings"? As I will discuss shortly, we are in the midst of a resurgence of theological readings of the Bible. There is, however, no general agreement among the growing tribe of theological interpreters of the Bible as to what precisely they are all doing. There are, of course, obvious family resemblances in the art of interpreting practiced by theologians such as David Ford,[2] David Kelsey,[3] and Michael Welker,[4] to name only three prominent figures. Yet even these three are sufficiently different from each other that my claim to be roughly in line with their approaches might not be entirely satisfying to those curious about what informs my own interpretive practice.

I am afraid, though, that I will have to disappoint those who seek an account of my method. I do not have anything that deserves to be called a "method" understood as a set of rules which, if followed, would always give the same, right result. Indeed, in an important sense, I am against "method." Of course, much of the theological reading of the Bible depends on the work of some academic disciplines with clear and compelling methodologies, such as the study of ancient languages and textual criticism. But when it comes to theological readings themselves, these are much more an art requiring wisdom than an exact science,[5] and there are

1. For a recent and very pluralistic post-modern proposal, see Dale B. Martin, *Pedagogy of the Bible. An Analysis and Proposal* (Louisville: Westminster John Knox, 2008).

2. See, for instance, David Ford, *Christian Wisdom: Desiring God and Learning in Love* (Cambridge: Cambridge University Press, 2007).

3. See David Kelsey, *Eccentric Existence: A Theological Anthropology* (Louisville: Westminster John Knox, 2009).

4. See, for instance, Michael Welker, *Creation and Reality* (trans. John F. Hoffmeyer; Minneapolis: Augsburg Fortress, 1999); Welker, *What Happens in Holy Communion?* (trans. John F. Hoffmeyer; Grand Rapids: Eerdmans, 2000); Welker, *God the Spirit* (trans. John F. Hoffmeyer; Minneapolis: Augsburg Fortress, 2004).

5. On wisdom in relation to reading the Bible see Kelsey, *Eccentric Existence*, 142-47.

many legitimate ways of reading the Scriptures. In my judgment, adherence to methods — let alone to a single method — unavoidably turns out to be unduly restrictive. Instead of following a strict method, I see myself engaged in an open-ended practice guided by convictions about the Bible (which themselves do suggest something like a set of maxims for reading well[6]). I will spell out these convictions below, but first I must address the broader issue of the relation of theologians to the Bible.

Theologians and the Bible

Ever since the Enlightenment, Christian academic theologians have had an ambivalent relationship to the Bible. On the one hand, after opening its pages they've often sensed they were entering a strange world. For instance, in the world of the Bible things don't happen just because mundane causes have effects, as in the "world" of the Enlightenment, but because God is actively engaged with the world; in this world "natural laws" yield to miraculous happenings, and the course of history is encompassed by God's providential government. Yawning wide between modern theologians and the ancient Bible was an "ugly broad ditch," to use a phrase of Gotthold Ephraim Lessing, one of the progenitors of the Enlightenment.[7] On the other hand, theologians continued to acknowledge that the Bible was the sacred text of the religious communities whose convictions, practices, and rituals they had devoted themselves to studying. And at least on occasion, theologians such as the young Karl Barth discovered for themselves that the "strange world" within the Bible is indeed a "strange *new* world," seemingly far outdated and yet peculiarly fresh, arresting, and life-giving.[8]

6. For examples of such rules see Ellen F. Davis and Richard B. Hays, eds., *The Art of Reading Scripture* (Grand Rapids: Eerdmans, 2003). An appropriation and adaptation of these rules can be found in Ford, *Christian Wisdom*.

7. Gotthold Ephraim Lessing, "On the Proof of the Spirit and of Power," in *Lessing's Theological Writings: Selections in Translation* (Stanford: Stanford University Press, 1957), 51-55.

8. See Karl Barth, "The Strange New World within the Bible," in *The Word of God and the Word of Man* (trans. Douglas Horton; New York: Harper & Brothers, 1957), 28-50. This

Considering these two opposing forces — the collision of the Bible with the "modern world" and the continued importance of the Bible for religious communities — it is not surprising that modern academic theology kept oscillating between an almost complete disregard of the Bible and a vigorous engagement with it. In either case, the Bible has been a difficult text for theologians: difficult to engage and difficult to abandon.

Whatever difficulties theologians face in engaging the Bible, these pale in comparison with the dangers of ignoring it. In fact, as I will argue below, disregarding the Bible is deadly for theology. This hazard is not the only reason for theology to re-engage the Bible, of course. It is not even the principal one, as though the main concern of theology were its self-perpetuation. In my judgment, Scripture is an indispensable and critical source of theological reflection because it is the primary site of God's self-revelation. At the center of Christian theology and Christian life in general is Jesus Christ, God's self-utterance to humanity, to use a phrase current a generation ago. The Bible is the primary and critical link of all subsequent generations to Jesus Christ. For Christians, Jesus Christ is the content of the Bible, and just for that reason the Bible is the site of God's self-revelation. I will have occasion to return briefly to God's self-revelation later, but now I turn to the dangers for theology in keeping the Bible at bay.

Theology as Scriptural Interpretation

It is well known that all the great theologians of the classical Christian tradition — from Origen and the Cappodocians to Augustine and Aquinas (to name just a few) — saw themselves as interpreters of the Scriptures. Summarizing a major thrust of Henri de Lubac's magisterial work *Medieval Exegesis,* Robert Wilken writes that for these theologians,

> biblical exegesis was not a specialized discipline carried on inde-
> pendently of theology; it *was* theology. The Church thought about

---

is a lecture Karl Barth delivered February 17, 1917, as he was writing what was to become the most consequential book for the course of twentieth-century theology — his interpretation of the apostle Paul's letter to the Romans (Karl Barth, *The Epistle to the Romans* [trans. Edwyn C. Hoskyns; New York: Oxford University Press, 1961]).

6

the mysteries of faith by expounding the text of the Bible. [. . .] Behind most theological discussions was a biblical text or texts, and it was on the basis of these texts that the Church's first teachers gave expression to the central truths of faith and morals.[9]

Not surprisingly, the same point about the centrality of scriptural interpretation in theology can be made by invoking any major figure from the Protestant Reformation. Martin Luther, for instance, famously rested his whole Reformation effort on the interpretation of the Scriptures guided by reason. As he declared before the emperor and other political and ecclesiastical dignitaries at the Diet of Worms: "Unless I am convinced by the testimony of the Scriptures or by clear reason [. . .], I am bound by the Scriptures I have quoted and my conscience is captive to the Word of God."[10] It is fitting that Luther's six-volume commentary on Genesis and two-volume commentary on Galatians — this last, my favorite of his texts — are likely the best and most complete expressions of his thought.[11]

At least since Immanuel Kant insisted in *Religion Within the Boundaries of Mere Reason* (1793) that philosophical theology "must have complete freedom to expand as far as its science reaches, provided that it stays within the boundaries of mere reason and makes indeed use of history, language, the books of the people, even the Bible, in order to confirm and explain its propositions,"[12] academic theologians, in the spirit of Kant — albeit against his explicit advice to theologians[13] — have been prone to do their work with little reference to the Bible. Friedrich Schleiermacher, the progenitor of modern theology and one of the great-

---

9. Robert Louis Wilken, "Foreword," in Henri de Lubac, *Medieval Exegesis,* Volume I: *The Four Senses of Scripture* (trans. Mark Sebanc; Grand Rapids: Eerdmans, 1998), x.

10. "Luther at the Diet of Worms," in *Luther's Works (LW)* (gen. eds. Jaroslav Pelikan and Helmut T. Lehmann; St. Louis: Concordia, 1955-86), 32:112.

11. Cf. Luther, *LW* vols. 1-6, and for Galatians see *LW* vols. 26-27. Heiko Oberman notes that Luther's lectures on Genesis, though fallen into oblivion, "deserve to be used as an introduction to Luther's world of faith" (Heiko Oberman, *Luther: Man Between God and the Devil* [trans. Eileen Walliser-Schwarzbart; New Haven: Yale University Press, 2006], 166-67).

12. Immanuel Kant, *Religion within the Boundaries of Mere Reason* (trans. and ed. Allen Wood and George di Giovanni; Cambridge: Cambridge University Press, 1998), 37.

13. Kant, *Religion within the Boundaries of Mere Reason,* 37.

est theologians ever, set the tone. His *The Christian Faith* contains virtually no exposition of the Bible.[14]

Still, as recently as the first half of the twentieth century some of the
most influential theologians continued to interpret biblical texts as an
essential part of their theological task.[15] (Or was it that they were influential in the long run precisely *because* they interpreted biblical texts?)
The most famous of such interpretive endeavors is Karl Barth's *The Epistle to the Romans*, the publication of which ushered in a veritable revolution in theology.[16] Throughout his career as a professor of theology,
Barth continued to teach the Bible and publish commentaries on biblical books, and he commented extensively on biblical texts in *Church
Dogmatics*, his magnum opus and, arguably, the greatest work of
twentieth-century theology. Similarly, most of Dietrich Bonhoeffer's ma-
ture work consisted of biblical exposition.[17] (His first two books were
published dissertations in which the Bible played a minor role.)

In the 1960s, a major shift occurred. From that time on, most of the
budding theologians no longer followed suit with Bonhoeffer or Barth, let
alone with Luther or Augustine. We need not examine here the conflu-
ence of factors that contributed to this momentous change, except to
note that it cannot be fully explained by the increased disciplinary and
subdisciplinary specialization characteristic of modern universities and
theological schools. Within an amazingly short period, systematic theologians finally "made good" on the early impulses received from Kant and
effectively gave up interpreting the Bible. Around the same time, and as
the culmination of a development that started during the Enlightenment,
many biblical scholars came to see themselves primarily as historians. A
wide chasm opened between the work of systematic theologians and biblical scholars: systematic theologians abandoned the Bible to biblical
scholars-turned-historians, and biblical scholars offloaded theology onto

14. Friedrich Schleiermacher, *The Christian Faith* (ed. and trans. H. R. Mackintosh
and J. S. Stewart; Philadelphia: Fortress, 1976).

15. Paul Tillich is likely the best example of a prominent theologian from the same
period who did *not* engage in a sustained interpretation of the Bible in his major works.

16. See footnote 8 above.

17. On Bonhoeffer as a biblical interpreter, see John Webster, *Holy Scripture: A Dogmatic Sketch* (Cambridge: Cambridge University Press, 2003), 78-85.

systematic theologians. The result? Locked into a distant past, the Bible became lost to the present, as far as academic theology was concerned.

The Price of Abandoning the Scriptures

Consider the consequences of pushing the Bible into the past in the light of the purposes of theology and the role of the Bible in Christian communities. As I understand it, the goal of academic theology, as distinct from religious studies, goes beyond striving to understand the world of the Christian faith. Theology seeks first to provide orientation to religious communities through critical and constructive engagement with their convictions, rituals, and practices — "to foster the knowledge and love of God" as the Yale Divinity School mission statement puts it. Second, theology's goal is to shape how life is lived in the broader society, indeed on the whole globe, in the light of God's purposes for the world. Church and society are the two main "publics" of academic theology,[18] those for whom it endeavors to interpret reality so as to offer guidance about what it means to live well before God.

What is the relation between theology's tasks with regard to these two publics? Consider that the majority of contemporary societies, including many Western ones, are culturally non-Christian. In a process that sociologists call "functional differentiation," social subsystems, such as economy and politics, have freed themselves from religious (which for all practical purposes means "Christian") claims and directives. Moreover, as a result of advancing globalization processes, most of the nations of the world — certainly most formerly "Christian" nations of the world — are becoming increasingly religiously pluralistic with no single religion dominating their cultural space.

Consider, too, that the effectiveness of Christian theology in a given social sphere is correlated with the vibrancy and potency of Christian religious language, rituals, and practices. Without such vibrancy and po-

18. There is also an "academic" public for theology, as David Tracy noted when he wrote that theology takes place in three publics — academy, society, and the church (see David Tracy, *Analogical Imagination: Christian Theology and the Culture of Pluralism* [New York: Crossroad, 1998], 3-46). This public is, in my judgment, a secondary one.

tency, academic theology for the most part spins its wheels without getting much traction. The consequence? In the absence of a robust "Christian culture" in functionally differentiated and religiously pluralistic societies, the influence of Christian theology in society is highly dependent on the role it plays in the churches and parachurch organizations where Christian religious language is alive and Christian practices are important. To the extent that theology is able to shape broader society at all, it will be able to do so *largely to the degree that it is able to shape the life of Christian communities.*[19]

Finally, note that Christian communities, to the extent that they are specifically Christian, are primarily nourished through the reading of the Bible, whether that reading occurs in liturgies, sermons, circles of friends, or private study. Certainly, Christian communities draw on other sources of nourishment as well — some of which provide them with spiritual junk food (such as pop-psychology), and others that yield solid nutrients (such as the responsible study of the human psyche, to stay with the same intellectual "food group"). They also draw on rich theological and spiritual traditions. But even the best of these sources — whether intra-Christian or extra-Christian — cannot substitute for the Scriptures. These others are important side-dishes; the Scriptures contain nutrients indispensable for the growth of individual Christians as well as ecclesiastical communities. The Scriptures represent the critical link to Jesus Christ as a site of God's self-revelation. Take the Scriptures away, and sooner or later you will "un-church" the Church.

If my descriptions of the role of the Scriptures in Christian communities and of the conditions of influence by academic theology in con-

---

19. The ideas, especially the ideas of scholars about religious convictions stemming from bygone eras, do not shape social realities today by floating freely in cyberspace or by sitting between the covers of books waiting for anyone interested to pick them up and do something with them. They do not shape realities even if they are carefully packaged and disseminated with the help of well-run publicity campaigns. Instead, ideas shape social realities when they are incarnated in social agents and communities of engagement, when they are the ideational side of actual or aspired ways of living. In the contemporary pluralistic world, with its relatively independent social subsystems, religious communities are by far the most likely candidates to serve as sites in which religious convictions can be incarnated, so that from there they can shape broader social environments.

temporary societies are correct, then the effects on both biblical studies and systematic theology of locking the Bible in the past are bound to be disastrous. Since the state of biblical studies today is not my concern here, I will only note that, under these conditions, a *merely historical* reading of biblical texts is in danger of turning into a self-referential study of inconsequential cultural artifacts from the distant past of a then insignificant corner of the world.[20] As I will stress again later, I do not mean to say that we should *not* study the Bible as a text from the past, but rather that such study of the Bible will be culturally and socially consequential largely to the extent to which the Bible is also and primarily read as Scripture, which is to say for its contemporary import.

As it turns out, even a clearly antiquarian study of biblical texts is often not perceived as being inconsequential. The reason is that actual interest in the work of biblical scholars as historians derives from the *present relation* that many people have to these texts. But remove the belief that the Bible has something to say to people today — as God's Word, as a wise or a harmful book, as a classic text, whatever — and interest in the pursuit and results of biblical studies will be negligible. The work of biblical scholars as historians is significant precisely to the degree that the texts which they approach as historians are alive today.

But no matter what the effect of treating the Bible as a merely historical document may be on biblical studies, for systematic theology to abandon the Bible is for it to cut off the branch on which it is sitting. All Christian theology that concerns the present — call it "systematic," "dogmatic," "constructive," or something else — must *ultimately* draw from the deep well of Scripture. True, fresh water can come from other sources too — reason, tradition, and experience, to name the three most frequently visited wells. Yet everything in theology that is specifically Christian finally derives from and is, in one way or another, measured by the content of the Scriptures, above all the Scriptures' witness to Jesus Christ. Moreover, if it abandons the Bible, Christian theology will no longer engage the document that lies at the heart of the life of Christian communities, the texts on

20. "The *raison d'être* of biblical studies, as distinct from the history of ancient Israel and early Christianity, is the belief that the biblical texts have something to say to the modern world," writes John J. Collins rightly ("Biblical Theology Between Apologetic and Criticism" [unpublished manuscript], 1).

which these communities depend for existence, identity, and vitality. The result will be a culturally and socially barren theology that hovers above concrete communities of faith — or maybe falls to the ground beside them — unable to shape either these communities or the wider culture.

Some might be tempted to read my argument for engaging the Scriptures theologically as a narrow, "back-to-the-Bible-fundamentalist" or at least peculiarly Protestant stance. It is not. *Any type of Christian theology* — "liberal" as well as "evangelical," "liberationist" no less than "conservative," Catholic and Orthodox and not only Protestant — will consign itself to a possibly slow but certain death if it is not nourished by the Scriptures. For all must go back to Scripture as their source of vitality and relevance; and none can ultimately bypass Scripture in coming to Jesus Christ, the cornerstone of the Christian faith. Granted, theologians will differ in how they read Scripture and what they find in it. The Jesus Christs of Jon Sobrino, Marcus Borg, and Pope Benedict XVI, to name just a few recent portrayals, are all rather different.[21] Yet they all go back to Scripture; none of them would have access to Jesus Christ at all if it were not for the reading of Scripture, and the debate about their accounts of Jesus Christ could not meaningfully take place without reference to the Scriptures.

Reflecting on his career as a theologian, Jürgen Moltmann, one of the most imaginative and influential theologians of the second part of the twentieth century, told me a decade or so ago that if he were to start over again, he would interpret the Scriptures in a much more sustained way. Why? Scripture is the ultimate source of theology's vigor, he said. He was right.

Resurgence of Engagement with Scripture

Many and diverse theologians share Moltmann's sense of the importance of scriptural interpretation for theology. Over the past two decades or so,

21. See, for instance, Jon Sobrino, *Jesus the Liberator* (Maryknoll, N.Y.: Orbis, 1993), and Sobrino, *Christ the Liberator* (Maryknoll, N.Y.: Orbis, 2001); Marcus Borg, *Jesus: A New Vision* (San Francisco: Harper & Row, 1987), and Borg, *Jesus: Uncovering the Life, Teachings, and Relevance of a Religious Revolutionary* (San Francisco: HarperSanFrancisco, 2006); Pope Benedict XVI, *Jesus of Nazareth* (trans. Adrian J. Walker; New York: Doubleday, 2007).

an explosion of interest in theological readings of the Scriptures occurred. Historians are studying biblical interpretations of classical theologians and publishing translations of major patristic and medieval commentaries on biblical texts;[22] biblical scholars are writing theological commentaries on biblical books[23] and are engaging in theological readings of biblical traditions;[24] systematic theologians are writing commentaries on biblical books,[25] offering extensive comments on biblical passages in their works,[26] and even crafting their whole theological projects as engagement with biblical traditions;[27] interfaith encounters, especially among the Abrahamic faiths, are being undertaken around joint readings of the scriptures of each tradition;[28] working groups and conferences consisting of biblical scholars and systematic theologians are being organized;[29] journals on theological scriptural interpretation are

22. For instance, *Ancient Christian Commentary on Scripture* (29 vols.; Downers Grove, Ill.: InterVarsity, 1998-).

23. For instance, J. Gordon McConville and Craig Bartholomew, eds., *The Two Horizons Old Testament Commentary* (Grand Rapids: Eerdmans, 2008-), and Joel B. Green and Max Turner, eds., *The Two Horizons New Testament Commentary* (Grand Rapids: Eerdmans, 2005-).

24. For instance, the work of Richard Bauckham, Ellen Davis, Richard Hays, Dale Martin, Marianne Meye Thompson, and N. T. Wright.

25. For instance, *Brazos Theological Commentary on the Bible* (Grand Rapids: Brazos, 2005-).

26. For instance, Kelsey, *Eccentric Existence.* My own work belongs in this category as well. See Miroslav Volf, *Exclusion and Embrace: Theological Reflections on Identity, Otherness, and Reconciliation* (Nashville: Abingdon, 1996), and Volf, *Free of Charge: Giving and Forgiving in a Culture Stripped of Grace* (Grand Rapids: Zondervan, 2005).

27. For instance, Friedrich Mildenberger, *Biblische Dogmatik: Eine biblische Theologie in dogmatischer Perspektive* (vols. 1-3; Stuttgart: Kohlhammer, 1991-93); Welker, *God the Spirit;* Welker, *Creation and Reality.*

28. A primary example of this is the Scriptural Reasoning group gathered around the work of Peter Ochs and David Ford, which I discuss later in this Introduction. See above all Peter Ochs, *Peirce, Pragmatism, and the Logic of Scripture* (Cambridge: Cambridge University Press, 1998); Ochs, ed., *Return to Scripture in Judaism and Christianity: Essays in Postcritical Scriptural Interpretation* (New York: Paulist, 1993); David Ford and C. C. Pecknold, eds., *The Promise of Scriptural Reasoning* (Malden, Mass.: Blackwell, 2006); *The Journal of Scriptural Reasoning* (http://etext.virginia.edu/journals/ssr/). See also Michael Ipgrave, ed., *Scriptures in Dialogue: Christians and Muslims Studying the Bible and the Qur'an Together* (London: Church House, 2004).

29. See, for instance, Davis and Hays, eds., *The Art of Reading Scripture;* and Markus

being published[30] and dictionaries on the same subject edited;[31] and even some secular philosophers are finding it worthwhile to wrestle anew with biblical writers.[32]

In my judgment, the return of biblical scholars to the theological reading of the Scriptures, and the return of systematic theologians to sustained engagement with the scriptural texts — in a phrase, the return of both to theological readings of the Bible — is *the most significant theological development in the last two decades.* Even if it is merely formal, it is comparable in importance to the post–World War I rediscovery of the Trinitarian nature of God[33] and to the resurgence of theological concern for the suffering and the poor in the late sixties of the past century.[34] Indeed, it can be argued that impulses from biblical texts were at the root of both of these rediscoveries.[35] True, because the Bible

---

Bockmuehl and Alan J. Torrance, eds., *Scripture's Doctrine and Theology's Bible: How the New Testament Shapes Christian Dogmatics* (Grand Rapids: Baker Academic, 2008).

30. For instance: *Ex Auditu: An International Journal for the Theological Interpretation of Scripture, Journal of Theological Interpretation,* and *Jahrbuch für biblische Theologie.*

31. Kevin J. Vanhoozer, ed., *Dictionary for Theological Interpretation of the Bible* (Grand Rapids: Baker Academic, 2005).

32. For example, Slavoj Žižek, *The Fragile Absolute, or Why Is the Christian Legacy Worth Fighting For?* (London: Verso, 2000). See also, Žižek, *The Puppet and the Dwarf: The Perverse Core of Christianity* (Cambridge, Mass.: MIT Press, 2003); Žižek, *On Belief* (London: Routledge, 2001); and Alain Badiou, *St. Paul: The Foundation of Universalism* (trans. Ray Brassier; Stanford: Stanford University Press, 2003).

33. Above all, Karl Barth, *Church Dogmatics* (ed. G. W. Bromiley and T. F. Torrance; Edinburgh: T. & T. Clark, 1957-67), vol. I; Karl Rahner, *The Trinity* (trans. Joseph Donceel; New York: Herder and Herder, 1970); Hans Urs von Balthasar, *Mysterium Paschale* (trans. Aidan Nichols; Edinburgh: T. & T. Clark, 1990); von Balthasar, *Theodramatik* (vols. 2 and 4; Einsiedeln: Johannes, 1976, 1983); von Balthasar, *Herrlichkeit: Eine theologische Ästhetik* (vols. 5 and 7; Einsiedeln: Johannes, 1961); and von Balthasar, *Theologik* (vol. 3; Einsiedeln: Johannes, 1987); Jürgen Moltmann, *The Crucified God: The Cross of Christ as the Foundation and Criticism of Christian Theology* (trans. R. A. Wilson and John Bowden; New York: Harper & Row, 1974), and Moltmann, *The Trinity and the Kingdom: The Doctrine of God* (trans. Margaret Kohl; New York: Harper & Row, 1981); Wolfhart Pannenberg, *Systematic Theology* (vol. 1; trans. Geoffrey W. Bromiley; Grand Rapids: Eerdmans, 1991), 259-336.

34. Foremost, Gustavo Gutiérrez, *A Theology of Liberation: History, Politics, and Salvation* (trans. and ed. Sister Caridad Inda and John Eagleson; Maryknoll, N.Y.: Orbis, 1973).

35. This is certainly true of Karl Barth, the original force behind the modern Trini-

can be misused and because it has been badly misused over the centuries, the value of rediscovering the theological reading of the Bible will ultimately depend on how well it is read. But still, its being read well depends on its being read in the first place.

Framework of Interpretation

With the essays published in this volume, as well as with *Exclusion and Embrace* and *Free of Charge* (and to a certain extent with *After Our Likeness* and *The End of Memory*),[36] I have participated in my own way in the renewal of interpreting the Bible theologically. As I read Scripture, I am guided by an integrated set of convictions about the Bible and its interpretation. In what follows, I will briefly explain these convictions, without being able to justify them fully or to show precisely how they inform the readings of biblical texts that I undertake in this volume.

Then and There

It may seem hackneyed to say that the Bible is a collection of texts written at particular times and places, each of them a text from then and there. Nevertheless, the consequences of this statement are far from

---

tarian resurgence. And this is also true of Jürgen Moltmann and Wolfhart Pannenberg, who, by going back to the biblical tradition of theology, offer two of the most compelling contemporary recastings of the doctrine of the Trinity (see Moltmann, *The Crucified God* and *The Trinity and the Kingdom;* Pannenberg, *Systematic Theology*). Arguably, all major liberation theologians have first drawn on the Exodus traditions and the Gospels, then read those traditions in the light of Marxist social analysis of Latin American societies, and, finally, offered reconstructions of theology. For an explicit engagement with biblical traditions by a liberation theologian, see José Miranda, *Marx and the Bible: A Critique of the Philosophy of Oppression* (trans. John Eagleson; Maryknoll, N.Y.: Orbis, 1974), and Miranda, *Communism in the Bible* (trans. Robert R. Barr; Eugene, Ore.: Wipf and Stock, 2004).

36. See Volf, *Exclusion and Embrace;* Volf, *Free of Charge;* Volf, *After Our Likeness: The Church as the Image of the Trinity* (Grand Rapids: Eerdmans, 1998); Volf, *The End of Memory: Remembering Rightly in a Violent World* (Grand Rapids: Eerdmans, 2008).

trite. It is therefore appropriate and necessary to study the Bible as a document from the past. Its reading is dependent on knowledge of the ancient languages in which it was originally written, and, all other things being equal, its interpretation is best undertaken against the backdrop of its multiple settings: economic, cultural, political, etc.

In addition to having been written in the past, the Bible, to a great extent, tells stories about concrete events from the past (narrated in a wide variety of literary genres and many containing very different implicit claims about whether and to what extent these narrated events actually took place). God is, arguably, its main character, and it is primarily about God's involvement — and, occasionally, apparent noninvolvement — with human beings in this-worldly events: in the doings and sufferings of the people of Israel, their ancestors, judges, kings, and prophets; in the life, death, and resurrection of Jesus Christ; in the mission of the apostles to establish and guide Christian churches.

The Bible is not principally a medium for communicating "religious wisdom," nor is it a record of atemporal epiphanic self-presentations of God, nor an account of happenings on another plane of existence alongside our own, nor a complex textual entity sketching an imaginative world the readers are invited somehow to inhabit. All these things — wisdom, epiphanies, happenings on a different plane of existence from our own, and imaginative worlds — are in the Bible, or the Bible can be construed to be partly about them. None of them, however, expresses the primary thrust of the Bible as a whole. Instead, it is primarily a document of God's involvement in "worldly" happenings in the past. I call this the "historicality" of the Bible (without committing myself thereby in any way to the modern notion of "historicity"). The Bible is therefore appropriately read as a narration of happenings, with an aim to understand what took place then and there and how what took place then and there was understood.[37] A theological reading will do more than that; it will also attend to what bearing these past happenings have on what needs to happen here and now. It should not do less.

The commitment to read the Bible as a witness to God's involvement

---

37. So rightly Francesca Murphy, *The Comedy of Revelation: Paradise Lost and Regained in Biblical Narrative* (Edinburgh: T&T Clark, 2000), xiv-xv.

in worldly happenings leaves open the question of what methods we should use to do so. Some argue that the historical-critical method — as formulated by Ernst Troeltsch and refined by those who followed in his trail[38] — is the only adequate tool. I very much doubt that.[39] To be used fruitfully in a theological reading of the Bible, the historical-critical method must, at minimum, shed its inherently secularizing bent and be redesigned to accommodate a worldview in which events are not adequately explained through reference to intra-mundane causalities.[40]

As theological readers of the Bible, however, we will very soon find ourselves bumping up against the limits of even a "refurbished" historical-critical method. As Søren Kierkegaard has argued in *Philosophical Fragments,* under the assumption that Jesus was God incarnate as the Christian tradition claims, even a hundred contemporary spies following Jesus' every move and noting every one of his miracles — let alone historians from a later period — would have missed this most important characteristic of his. The reason is very simple and obvious: notwithstanding powerful and pervasive metaphorical language in the Bible and theology about "hearing," "seeing," and even "tasting" God, God is by definition inaccessible to our senses, as most Christian theologians agree.[41] And if God is the main character of the Bible as a whole, Kierkegaard's argument applies more broadly than just to the life of Jesus. Using a redesigned historical-critical method, we might be able to

38. See Ernst Troeltsch, "Historische und Dogmatische Methode in der Theologie," in *Gesammelte Schriften von Ernst Troeltsch* (Aalen: Scentia, 1962), 2:729-53.

39. I fully agree with Dale Martin that the historical character of Christianity as a religion does not make the historical-critical method an indispensable tool for interpreting biblical texts. Those who make this claim confuse the two meanings of historical — one having to do with past events and the other having to do with methods of modern historiography (Martin, *Pedagogy of the Bible,* 40-44).

40. See, for instance, Wolfhart Pannenberg, *Jesus — God and Man* (trans. Lewis L. Wilkins and Duane A. Priebe; Philadelphia: Westminster, 1968), 21-37. See also Walter Kasper, *Jesus the Christ* (trans. V. Green; New York: Paulist, 1976), 15-61.

41. According to Kierkegaard, a person contemporaneous with Jesus would have derived no significant epistemological advantage over a person from a later time, because, if the contemporary "believes his eyes, he is deceived, for the God is not immediately knowable" (Søren Kierkegaard, *Philosophical Fragments* [trans. David F. Swenson and Howard V. Hong; Princeton: Princeton University Press, 1962], 78).

make a plausible argument that a man spoke certain unusual words or that a woman was healed, but not that these words were *divinely* inspired or that *God* had anything to do with the healing. For we cannot legitimately conclude that God was at work in what we are unable to explain.[42]

This, of course, does not settle the question of whether God was indeed at work in the grand story and all the little stories that the Bible narrates. It simply contends that *if* God was at work, then the Bible, precisely as a witness to the happenings from the past, must be read in a particular way for these happenings to be understood for what they in fact were. That was Kierkegaard's point. The reminder that God is inaccessible to our senses also underscores that the fundamental question of whether or not God was at work in the biblical stories cannot be answered by a historian *qua* historian using a historical-critical method of any sort, because it involves matters of a metaphysical and theological nature; to find God in the Bible, one has to presuppose God in the Bible — hopefully not arbitrarily, but on good grounds.[43]

Here and Now

As a collection of texts from the past about events in the past (primarily), the Bible is also a *book for today.* At one level, this is a descriptive claim: the Bible is the most translated, most widely circulated, and most widely read book in the history of humanity. Clearly, people of all ages and places have continued to find in it something of great importance. Given the dynamic growth of Christianity worldwide — contemporary Western

42. With somewhat different intent from mine here, Langdon Gilkey made a similar argument many years ago with regard to the Exodus: in principle, historical science could not establish that the Exodus was an act of God even if science did establish that it happened (Langdon Gilkey, "Cosmology, Ontology, and the Travail of Biblical Language," *Journal of Religion* 41 [1961]: 194-205).

43. The consequence of this is that a historian *qua* historian cannot make a valid judgment about the most basic and momentous feature of the Bible, namely, the claim that God is at work in human history — most particularly, in the person of Jesus of Nazareth.

Europe being a notable exception — this is not likely to change any time soon.

At another level, saying that the Bible is a book for today is a normative claim: it is a kind of book that *ought* to be read today. Why? One answer — not central to my main purpose here, though I will return to it briefly at the end when I discuss non-Christian readings of the Bible — is that the Bible is a *classic spiritual* text, in fact, *the* classic text of many cultures profoundly influenced by Christianity. Over the past two thousand years the Bible has shaped the cultures of Europe, the Americas, Australia, and many other parts of the world more than any other text. Even today, at the beginning of the third millennium, in media-saturated cultures moving at a frantic pace when many bemoan the serious decline in religious literacy, contemporary Western societies continue to rest on "cultural capital" inherited from the Bible.[44] Without familiarity with the Bible and the history of its cultural influences, the knowledge of our own cultural past and present will lose depth. Similarly, if we do not engage this formative text, we will lose a significant source of cultural orientation. That is reason enough to read the Bible for its import for us today, study its wide-ranging cultural effects over the course of history, and above all wrestle seriously with its accounts of who human beings are and what it means to live well.

More important for my purposes here, the Bible is a *sacred* text (and it has become a classic text chiefly *because* it is a sacred text). It is held to be Holy Scripture by the Christian churches (and, of course, a significant

---

44. We can even say that Western cultures are "soaked through with the cultural substance of the Bible" (Michael Welker, "What Is Biblical Theology?" [unpublished manuscript], 12), even if it is true that most of their inhabitants are unaware of the Christian origins and the necessity for religious grounding of some of their deep convictions, such as the embrace of human rights (see Nicholas Wolterstorff, *Justice: Rights and Wrongs* [Princeton: Princeton University Press, 2008]; John Witte Jr., *The Reformation of Rights* [Grand Rapids: Eerdmans, 2006]). This is not to say that Western cultures are not getting increasingly de-Christianized. Those who live in them may embrace fully the language of human rights but be completely unaware of their Christian derivation, and reject both Christian grounding of these rights and the need for religious motivations to respect them (see Richard Rorty, "Human Rights, Rationality, and Sentimentality," in *On Human Rights: The Oxford Amnesty Lectures* [ed. Stephen Shute and Susan Hurley; New York: Basic Books, 1993], 111-34).

portion of it is also considered Holy Scripture by Jews), a witness to God's involvement with the world, and a site of God's self-revelation.[45] The Bible exists as Holy Scripture because the Christian churches exist (and, of course, the Christian churches exist because the Bible exists as the Holy Scripture). Here we do not need to delve into all the intricacies of the relationship between the Bible and the Church as it has been explored, for instance, in the centuries-long debates between Catholic and Protestant positions. It suffices to note that the contemporaneity of the Bible as well as the predominant Christian strategies of reading the Bible (for example, giving the texts within a canon an overarching reading) are to a significant degree a consequence of the Bible's being the Holy Scripture of Christian communities.

For the Bible to be the sacred text of the Christian communities means, at minimum, that it is not merely a witness to how God as its main character acted in the particularities of the past events narrated, but also a medium of God's involvement in the lives of people today — maybe a bit like a historical drama performed before a live audience,[46] though designed to address more immediately each reader and every human being than dramas normally do.

It is, however, not just that the Bible speaks to us today by narrating events from the past (and thereby eliciting our identification with or distancing from the stories told and, as a sacred text, claiming our identification with its story, our embrace of its account of God and God's dealings with humanity, and our obedience to its commands). For today's

---

45. To say that the Bible is "a site of God's self-revelation" can be understood in many different ways. With Nicholas Wolterstorff we could see it, for instance, as divinely appropriated human discourse (*Divine Discourse: Philosophical Reflections on the Claim That God Speaks* [Cambridge: Cambridge University Press, 1995]). Or with John Webster we can understand biblical texts as "creaturely realities set apart by the triune God to serve his self-presence" (*Holy Scripture*, 21). Options are many, and my purpose in this section is not to discuss various options, but to underscore that treating the Bible as a site of God's self-revelation is one significant commitment of my theological reading of the Bible. As it will become manifest shortly, I embrace a position close to Wolterstorff's, and the commitment to this particular "ontology" of the Bible influences significantly the way I think the Bible ought to be read.

46. See Robert Jenson, "Scripture's Authority in the Church," in Davis and Hays, eds., *The Art of Reading Scripture*, 30-34.

readers are not outside the events the Bible is narrating, acquiescing to being pulled or resisting being pulled into those events by the power of the narrative. The readers — whether Christian or not, whether named as addressees or not — are *in* these events. When we read at the very beginning of the Bible, "Let us make humankind in our image" (Gen. 1:26), we are involved. When John the Evangelist writes, "The true light, which enlightens everyone, was coming into the world" (John 1:9), all readers are included. When the apostle Paul writes in 2 Corinthians, "one died for all; therefore all have died" (5:14), something significant is asserted about every potential reader of the Bible. And when we read at the very end of the Bible, "See, the home of God is among mortals. He will dwell with them; they will be his people, and God himself will be with them" (Rev. 21:3), we ourselves are those mortals to whom the promise is given. The Bible is about all of us — about who we are and what has happened or will happen to us, and about what it means for us to live well. Within its story the Bible tells the story of humanity and each person in it.

Whether seen as a classic text or a sacred text through which God speaks, the Bible is a book for today. At minimum that requires theologians to attend to and wrestle with the broad contours as well as the details of the vision of the relations between God and humanity that the Bible lays out. It will not suffice to analyze the texts and their authors and recipients as "phenomena" — as the world *of* the texts, *behind* the texts, or *in front of* the texts. In a recent lecture Moltmann makes this point with the help of an analogy. He sketches what he describes as a "nightmare" scenario involving himself:

> I imagine that I step behind the pulpit in a church and preach in order to proclaim the Gospel and, if possible, awaken the faith. But those who sit in the pew don't listen to my words. A historian is there who examines critically facts about which I am speaking; a psychologist is there who analyzes my psyche which reveals itself in my speech; a cultural anthropologist is there who observes my personal style; a sociologist is there who is identifying the class to which I belong and as whose representative he believes I am functioning. Everybody is analyzing me and my context, but nobody is listening to what I want to say. And the worst thing is:

nobody is disagreeing with me, nobody wants to discuss with me what I have just said.[47]

With the self-confessed exaggeration of a good caricaturist, Moltmann sketches the contrast between "wrestling" with the messages of the Bible and what might be described as the "analytical domestication" of the Bible: a kind of condescending endeavor to understand biblical writers better than they understood themselves and thereby dismiss what they wanted to say. In principle, there is no reason, of course, why the analysis of texts, authors, and recipients cannot be placed in the service of wrestling with the message of the Bible, but the thrust of Moltmann's comment is well taken. If the Bible were merely a book from the past about the past, it might be appropriate to limit ourselves to studying its history and its multiple contexts, exploring its authors' and recipients' possible backgrounds and features, or comparing similarities to and differences from other texts and tracing possible influences between biblical and non-biblical ideas, and so on. But since the Bible is a book for today, we need to understand its multiple and multiform claims, identify what they may have to say to us, and wrestle responsibly with them.[48]

Unity and Diversity

The Bible is, obviously, not a single book with many interrelated parts (at least not a single book in the ordinary sense), but a collection of books, a "pluralistic library," as someone has called it. Yet it also forms a unity; it is a certain "kind of whole."[49] I do not mean that the library called "The Holy Bi-

47. Jürgen Moltmann, "'Do you understand what you are reading?' New Testament Scholarship and the Hermeneutical Question of Theology" (unpublished manuscript in German; my translation), 8-9.

48. An interpreter is likely to experience a tension between the "historicality" and "contemporaneity" of the Bible. A character of a particular theological reading of biblical texts will be shaped greatly by how an interpreter deals with this tension. Considering that I am offering here a mere sketch of my basic interpretive convictions, I will leave undiscussed the multiple ways in which a theological reading can hold together both the Bible's historicality and contemporaneity.

49. Kelsey, *Eccentric Existence*, 148, 458-77.

ble" is a unity merely in the way that the library called "The Yale University Sterling Memorial Library" is a unity simply by existing at a particular location and therefore being one entity rather than many. Neither do I mean that the Bible is unified merely by functioning as a canon — a collection of the particular books in it, as opposed to a collection of other books that might have been considered authoritative for Christian communities. Both of these forms of unity are *external,* either holding diverse texts together between two covers or asserting a unique relationship between readers and a particular selection of texts as distinct from a different selection.

I take it, perhaps controversially, that the Bible as a collection of texts deemed canonical by Christian communities, also has an *internal unity.* When you read this particular collection of texts as a whole, without being sidetracked by its many and diverse side-plots and excurses (sometimes consisting of entire books), it tells a single basic story.[50] Consider the story that structures a single book of the Bible, John's Gospel. The words with which the Gospel begins — "In the beginning was the Word" (John 1:1) — echo the opening words of the Bible as the whole — "In the beginning, God created the heavens and the earth" (Gen. 1:1). (At the same time John's words refer to events that "precede" the beginning of which we read in Genesis.) The Gospel ends with the words, "until I come" (John 21:23), a reference to Christ's "second coming," which corresponds to the prayer, "Come, Lord Jesus!" at the very end of the very last book of the Bible (Rev. 22:20).[51] In the middle the Gospel tells of God's presence in the life and person of Jesus as he was teaching, healing the sick and feeding the hungry, washing the feet of his disciples, bearing "away the sin of the world" as the Lamb of God (John 1:30), and, as the Resurrected One, sending the disciples into the world as he himself was sent.

---

50. It may be a complex story, made up of elements that are factually intertwined but logically separable (as David Kelsey has argued about the story of God's relation to humanity in *Eccentric Existence*), but it is nonetheless recognizably a single story. On "story" as uniting the Bible see, among many others, Richard Bauckham, "Reading Scripture as a Coherent Story," in Davis and Hays, eds., *The Art of Reading Scripture,* 38-53; N. T. Wright, "Reading Paul, Thinking Scripture," in Bockmuehl and Torrance, eds., *Scripture's Doctrine,* 59-71.

51. See Bauckham, "Reading Scripture as a Coherent Story," in Davis and Hays, eds., *The Art of Reading Scripture,* 41.

Now the same story that unites the Gospel of John unites "The Holy Scripture Library" as well. That this is so is less obvious because the large swaths of what Christians describe as the Old Testament seemingly have nothing to do with Jesus Christ. Yet as part of the Christian canon, the Old Testament along with the New is brought to unity as part of the story of Jesus Christ. The story that structures both John's Gospel and the Bible as a whole is the story captured well by the early Christian "Apostles' Creed" — a foundational text for the self-understanding of the majority of Christian churches (whether it is recited as part of their liturgies or not).

Contained between the covers of the Bible and held together by the contours of that single and brief overarching story, however, is an *astonishing diversity* of voices speaking from a remarkable variety of perspectives that resist all attempts at harmonizing. I take this diversity to be a direct result of the historicality of God's self-revelation, of the fact that the Bible is about God speaking and acting in given times and spaces, addressing people living in distinct cultures, shaped by individual histories and the specific convergence of influences, beset by diverse concrete problems, and carried on the wings of many distinct hopes. This diversity is, in a sense, an echo of the complexity and fluidity of the created human life itself as it has been lived over the centuries in which the various biblical texts were composed and redacted. The content of the Bible cannot be fitted into a coherent "system" in the way that, say, various pieces of a puzzle may be fitted together because they were designed in advance to fit.[52] The task of maintaining the tensions of this diversity within a coherent whole may seem a bit like forging a euphonious or-

---

52. As many have observed, there is something profoundly odd about fundamentalist attempts to show that all the claims of the Bible fit into a coherent system. Reverence for the Bible drives the whole project — God's Word does not contradict itself because God does not make self-contradictory statements — and yet irreverence for the concrete claims of the Bible is often enacted by squeezing them to fit into a system. As Robert H. Gundry, who himself advocates a rather traditional Protestant view of biblical inspiration, has noted, biblical texts are not "tailored for the sake of suprahistorical comprehensiveness (producing a unifiedly systematic theology) but for the sake of intrahistorical pertinence" (Robert H. Gundry, "Hermeneutic Liberty, Theological Diversity, and Historical Occasionalism," in *The Old Is Better: New Testament Essays in Support of Traditional Interpretations* [Tübingen: Mohr Siebeck, 2005], 17).

chestra out of a motley crew of musicians, each inspired from the same source and yet none playing by a written score.

Yet the rich polyphony contained in the Bible — harmonious as well as discordant — is its strength, not its weakness. It makes the Bible alive — a witness to God's speaking and acting at various points into the dynamics of life, capable of being "translated" into a wide variety of situations today.

Truthful theological readings of the Bible will always seek to honor both the overarching story, which gives the Bible its unity, and the concrete character of its diverse specific texts. To respect the integrity of both at the same time is difficult, as any attentive reader of biblical texts knows. Yet precisely as a sacred text, the Bible will speak today in an authentic voice only if we situate our readings in the tension between its overarching unity and its sometimes bewildering diversity.

Meaning

Place the Bible in the hands of contemporary readers, and its rich diversity turns into an even richer multivocality. Every single one of its diverse texts will show itself as having multiple meanings.

It is commonplace today to say that discrete biblical texts or text-segments do not have a single meaning. Not so long ago, biblical scholars and theologians alike would have strenuously contested this claim. As least since the time of the great European humanists, the belief was widespread that biblical texts did have a single meaning, often identified with what the original writer (or redactor) of the text intended to say. We can leave aside here the question of whether a theory that lodges the meaning of texts solely in the minds of their writers and claims that texts have a single meaning is plausible as a general hermeneutical approach.[53] The question for us is whether, to what extent, and in what ways it applies specifically to the text of the Bible, understood above all as a sacred text for all times and places. In regard to single vs. plural

---

53. For a classical defense of this position, see E. D. Hirsch Jr., *Validity in Interpretation* (New Haven: Yale University Press, 1967).

meanings of a text, my position, which I can only sketch here in outline, is that biblical texts have a multiplicity of legitimate meanings. The rejection of a single-meaning approach is tied to the convictions that the Bible is a site of God's self-revelation and that the texts comprise God's word addressed to people of all times and places.

Ibn 'Arabi (1165-1240), the great Sufi theologian, wrote in regard to reciting the Qur'an: "When meaning repeats itself for someone who is reciting the Qur'an, he has not recited it as it should be recited. This is proof of his ignorance."[54] The same, I think, applies to reading the Christian Bible. To see why and how this might be the case, recall the saying of the ancient Greek philosopher Heraclitus: "As they step in the same rivers, different and (still) different waters flow upon them."[55] Analogously, a biblical text cannot "speak" the same thing to the same person twice. For when it "speaks" the second time, the hearer (reader), caught inescapably in the ever-changing flux of life, will have changed, and will therefore be unable to hear the same words in exactly the same way. Moreover, it is not really the text that speaks. Texts aren't speakers. In the Bible, understood as the site of God's self-revelation, it is God who speaks. Though never-changing in God's own being, God is actively present to all times and places. The consequence? As the life of the hearer/reader changes, the meaning of the biblical text changes. The well is inexhaustible, and the ever-fresh water of God is flowing from it to people whose lives are defined by constant change. In Heraclitus's terms,[56] neither the divine river nor the people who come to it for the living water are ever the same. The diversity of biblical traditions and the diversity of their meanings are both rooted in the same phenomenon: the fact that

---

54. Quoted in William C. Chittick, *Ibn 'Arabi: Heir to the Prophets* (Oxford: Oneworld, 2007), 18.

55. Heraclitus, *Fragments: A Text and Translation with a Commentary by T. M. Robinson* (Toronto: University of Toronto Press, 1987), 17.

56. I am interpreting Heraclitus along the lines of Plato, as advocating the position that "all things are in movement and nothing stays put" (Plato, *Cratylus* [Loeb Classical Library, vol. IV; trans. H. N. Fowler; Cambridge, Mass.: Harvard University Press, 1926], 402a), so that the reason why one cannot step into the same river twice is that both the river and the person are caught in change. Obviously, "change" in the divine well is change connected with the God who is utterly faithful and possesses plenitude of being.

they are modes of engagement of the infinitely rich God with multiple, diverse, and dynamic creatures.

Should we conclude, then, that *anything* goes when it comes to readings of the Bible? Are there no constraints to multiplying meanings? Are we to believe that the Bible not only often is, but is doomed always to remain a wax nose, to be bent in whichever direction we deem useful or interesting? If so, we would find ourselves in a dangerous situation. The Bible is a potent text, and over the past two thousand years it has been interpreted in seriously nefarious ways. So we have a political as well as a religious stake in maintaining constraints on the meaning of biblical texts.[57]

Sufficiently imaginative minds can interpret texts to mean virtually anything. Unlike speakers who feel that listeners have misinterpreted them, texts themselves are inert and cannot protest or correct the interpreter. Yet protests and corrections do occur. Multiple readers contend among themselves as to the plausibility of a given reading. To what must the contending readers ultimately appeal as they spar about which readings are more plausible? To the features of the texts considered in a given literary context[58] and, for theological readings, also considered in the context of the overarching narrative that gives the Bible its unity. They will likely consult and rely on various authorities, such as compelling saints, seminal scholars, longstanding traditions of communal interpretation, or, for some, official teaching offices of the church. But ultimately the features of the text will have the "final say" in the interpretation of those texts.

And why is there anything to argue about in the first place? Why not

57. The same holds true for sacred texts of other religions. The debate about proper rules of interpretation and "legitimate" ways of harvesting the meaning of a text such as the Qur'an, for instance, is of great importance for Muslim communities themselves, as well as for all Muslims' neighbors. On rules of interpreting the Qur'an, see for example Ghazi bin Muhammad bin Talal, "General Editor's Introduction and Foreword," in *Tafsir al-Jalalayn* (Louisville: Fons Vitae, 2008).

58. The proper context for interpreting any given text will be strenuously debated. "The context in terms of which a unit of literature is to be interpreted is never self-evident," writes Jon Levenson rightly in his famous essay "Why Jews Are Not Interested in Biblical Theology" (in Jon Levenson, *The Hebrew Bible, the Old Testament, and Historical Criticism* [Louisville: Westminster John Knox, 1993], 56).

simply note the different purposes and interests of diverse readers and celebrate the diversity of interpretations? This question takes us to the relation between texts and meanings. "Texts don't mean; people mean with texts," writes Dale Martin, describing what he calls one of his "favorite slogans."[59] I agree, with qualification. Texts are not agents and therefore do not "mean" in the sense of "intending to signify something." Yet texts are also not like things in a world without God, dependent on our interpretation for their meaning. Instead, like created realities in classical Christian theology, they have *inherent* meanings. They mean roughly the way "scripture" *means* "any writing considered by a community to be sacred."[60] Why? For the most part, texts are products of the intentional — though never fully controlled — activity of encoding meanings so as to communicate something to somebody else. Communication among people is possible because the activity of encoding meanings is institutionalized in the form of sign systems, which themselves must be understood together with "their extra-systemic references to what is perceived and intended."[61]

One way to make my point is to say that while texts are not agents, they are not things either. *Texts are social relations* — in a sense similar to a gift's not being a thing but a social relation,[62] or, in Marx's analysis, to a commodity's not being a thing but a social relation.[63] A thing is a gift only when it is part of a social relation in which somebody gives something to somebody else; words, sentences, and paragraphs are a "text" when we understand them as something crafted by someone in order to say (and, more broadly, to do) something to somebody else. To relate to texts while abstracting from their and one's own relation to their au-

59. Martin, *Pedagogy,* 31.

60. Terry Eagleton has distinguished rightly between two senses of "meaning" (and has related the two) — "meaning as a given signification and meaning as an act which intends to signify something" (*The Meaning of Life* [Oxford: Oxford University Press, 2007], 59).

61. So rightly Hans Joas (*Do We Need Religion? On the Experience of Self-Transcendence* [Boulder: Paradigm, 2008], 40), reporting on the work of Cornelius Castoriadis.

62. For a brief discussion of gift as a social relation see Miroslav Volf, *Free of Charge,* 55-58.

63. See Karl Marx, *Das Kapital: Kritik der politischen Oekonomie* (Hamburg: O. Meissner, 1872-94), 1:9-61.

thors' intentions and interests in writing them is to treat them as mere things; it is to commit what one may call "text fetishism," a fallacy not too dissimilar to what Marx called "commodity fetishism."[64]

Two important consequences follow from treating texts as social relations with encoded meanings. First, if the meanings are encoded in them, the reader is not called to the endeavor of the "making of meaning,"[65] as though none were encoded in the text, but rather to the task of "decoding meaning(s)," or, more precisely, constructing plausible accounts of the meanings encoded. Even individual words are not "just dead husks waiting to have meaning breathed into them by live speakers," Terry Eagleton has rightly observed; much less is that the case with whole texts.[66] At the same time, just as a gift in most cases needs to be received

64. Marx, *Das Kapital,* 46-50, esp. 47-50.

65. Martin, *Pedagogy,* 30.

66. Eagleton, *Meaning of Life,* 61. The theory of meaning which claims that it is we who invest a literary text with meaning rather than meaning's already being embedded in it Eagleton describes, rightly, as "troublingly narcissistic" and asks rhetorically, "Do we never get outside our own heads?" (p. 116). To guard against narcissism in relation to texts, it is essential not to understand interpretation *as* use, but to distinguish categorically between "interpretation" of texts and multiple "uses" to which we can put them. Richard Rorty, against whom one may compellingly level Eagleton's kind of charge of narcissism, disagrees. He thinks that the distinction between interpretation and use is problematic. He dismisses the Aristotelian contrast between theory and practice and the Kantian contrast between merely using persons as means and treating them as ends in themselves. The Aristotelian epistemological and Kantian ethical contrasts, Rorty believes, are wrongheaded, and they undergird a mistaken hermeneutical distinction between interpretation and use. Continuing with the argument, Rorty goes on to suggest a more fruitful hermeneutical distinction within the overarching hermeneutical affirmation of interpretation as use, which is the one "between knowing what you want to get out of a person or a thing or a text in advance and hoping that the person or thing or text will help you want something different — that he or she or it will help you change your purposes, and thus change your life" (Richard Rorty, "The Pragmatist's Progress," in *Interpretation and Overinterpretation* [ed. Umberto Eco and Stefan Collini; Cambridge: Cambridge University Press, 1992], 106). Rorty's explanation, though seemingly weakening the force of the charge of narcissism, in fact strengthens it. I will not comment here on Rorty's dismissal of the Aristotelian practice-theory contrast, even though it is fundamental, but zero in on his rejection of the Kantian means-ends contrast, which is more pertinent to the issue at hand. The critical question is not, as it was for Kant in relation to persons, whether we are allowed merely to use texts or not; texts are not persons, and they can be legitimately used. The critical question is

as a gift to be effectively given, so also a text needs to be decoded — received as encoded meaning — to mean something to somebody actively.

Second, encodings are always encodings of one thing, however polysemous, rather than another; therefore they always place constraints on plausible construals of the meaning encoded. It is *possible,* for instance, to interpret "For God so loved the world . . ." as an attempt by an evil genius to lull people into thinking that God cares for the world so as to be able all the more easily to destroy it. But very few would consider this a *plausible* reading of that statement in John's Gospel. Why? Not because these words *cannot* mean what I just suggested they could. Obviously, they can (and a Nietzschean of a certain sort might even defend this interpretation). But the narrative and theological context of the third chapter of John's Gospel, the rest of the Gospel account, the entire New Testament, and the Christian Bible as a whole make that interpretation, arguably, implausible.

Jeffrey Stout has suggested that we may be better off substituting for the phrase "plausible accounts of multiple meanings" the designation "interesting readings" (in the sense of serving "our interests and purposes" as

---

whether *interpretation* is properly pursued as "use of texts as mere means." It is not — precisely because texts, though not persons, are not simply things either, as I have suggested above. You can treat texts as things — as self-standing human artifacts that one uses — and this is very much a legitimate relation of a reader to texts, at least to many of them. But as things, texts are also and first of all social relations — somebody is communicating something to somebody else by their means. In this regard, reading texts is not unlike receiving gifts, which also are not mere things but social relations, "somethings" whose character is defined by being that which someone is imparting to someone else. Rorty cuts off the "imparting someone" from the interpretative process and casts interpretation as one-sided taking or being affected — I take from the text what I am interested in taking or I let the text affect me (though the latter is completely unrelated to what the author of the text wanted to achieve with it). This is signaled by the term "use." And this is also where narcissism creeps in. The idea of texts' helping you think differently or be a different person does not fundamentally take you out of yourself because it is about what you want and allow the texts to do for you. This is underscored by the empty notion of difference in Rorty's text, which is completely referenced to the reader's interests and purposes. Hermeneutical process seems tailor-made for the cultural space whose imagination is dominated by self-interest, whether self-interest is pursued in the form of mercantile exchange or more general experiential satisfaction, including the satisfaction of being different today from yesterday.

well as of being interesting to us).[67] The suggestion will not work, I think, if I am correct that texts are not mere things but social relations in which someone says something to someone else with the help of a shared sign system. The suggestion seems to me positively mistaken when it comes to texts in which readers are *directly* addressed, and doubly so if the texts in which readers are directly addressed are the sacred texts.

I don't normally open a letter that a friend has written to me in order to come up with an interesting reading of it, not even a long letter of a very geeky friend in which multiple genres are employed — poems, stories, parables, proverbs. Neither do I read the letter primarily to pursue some personal interest, except an interest in honoring our friendship by trying to figure out what that friend wanted to communicate by writing the letter to me (however complex and multilayered the intention may have been).[68] I may decide that what my friend wrote is interesting (and possibly reread the letter multiple times), and I may then pursue some interests of my own in offering him or someone else an interesting reading of the letter. But all that comes *after* I have found out what my friend wanted to say (or, if the letter is complex, constructed a plausible account of what he wanted to say). I honor a writer of a letter addressed to me by taking seriously *the writer's* interest to communicate something to me, and therefore by trying to figure out, as best as I can, what it is that

67. Jeffrey Stout, "What Is the Meaning of a Text?" *New Literary History* 14/1 (1982): 1-12.

68. For example, when Cicero writes to Atticus, "The state of things in regard to my candidature, in which I know you are supremely interested, is this . . . ," I take it that he expects Atticus to read his letter and figure out how it is that Cicero understands "the state of things in regard to his candidature," and indeed that Atticus would have some moral obligation to do so even if he were not "supremely interested" in the matter (Marcus Tullius Cicero, *Letters to Atticus* [trans. D. R. Shackleton Bailey [New York: Cambridge University Press, 1965], 1:1-2; Cicero, *Letters of Marcus Tullius Cicero, with his treatises on friendship and old age* [trans. E. S. Shuckburgh; New York: P. F. Collier & Son Co., 1917]). Now it may be true that these letters were published later for the literary public in order to display Cicero's literary acumen and political wisdom to contemporaries and to posterity (as suggested by Marcus Elder, who invoked this example in private correspondence with me). So both Atticus and the literary public are addressed. Yet I would argue that Atticus has a moral obligation to figure out what Cicero is trying to say and to respond to him, whereas the literary public has no obligation whatsoever to pay any attention to what Cicero has written or published.

the writer wanted to say. I dishonor such a writer if I fail to do that.[69] Before my interests and purposes in reading and interpreting come into play, I have a *moral obligation* to the writer that arises from the particular social relation created by his writing a letter to me.

As it is with a letter addressed to me, so it is with the Bible read theologically — provided we understand the Bible as the Holy Scripture, a site of God's self-disclosure and its various texts as media of God's speech to us today.[70] As Holy Scripture, the Bible is not only a classic of world literature. One can legitimately treat classics as texts floating in "human space" addressed to all people and only indirectly to each person. Consequently, one may engage or not engage them, depending on one's proclivities and preferences, and read them in the light of one's interests and purposes (though when a person does so, the danger of narcissism may never be far). Even though the Bible is a classic of spiritual literature, to a theological reader it is like a letter — always addressed directly to each human being and therefore obliging us to read it with the goal of finding its authors' interests and purposes.

Stance

Many people today, especially scholars, approach the Bible with suspicion. This is not surprising. For one thing, we are modern men and

---

69. Stout has suggested that we would be better off not using the term "meaning" at all, though he agrees there is no harm in doing so, as long as we specify what we mean by the term. For my part, I don't mind dropping the talk of "meaning," provided I can keep the language, "what the author intended to communicate."

70. None of this is to say that a person cannot profit by putting aside completely the idea that through the text of the Bible God speaks to each human being today, so that one can read the Bible for his or her own chosen "interests and purposes" — whatever these interests and purposes may be, and whether leaning on Marx, Nietzsche, Freud, or somebody else for interpretation and inspiration. It is also not to say that such readings are always inappropriate when it comes to the Bible. It is just that such readings *would* be appropriate at only *one* level of what these texts are — literary products from diverse times and places that have acquired the status of potent classics. But such readings miss what is theologically and, more broadly, Christianly, the most important thing about the Bible: namely, that it is the Word of God addressed to people of all times and places.

women, individuals standing on our own two feet, masters and mistresses of our own choices and destinies — or so we like to think. For others to insert us into their story and envision the proper end of our lives, define for us the source and substance of human flourishing, and tell us what we should or should not desire, is for them to violate us as self-standing individuals. The Bible as a sacred text, however, does just that.

Second, the Bible has a long history of misuse. The powerful employ it as a weapon against the weak, whether these are the poor or women or any socially excluded group (as per a historically influential though mistaken interpretation of Karl Marx[71]). The weak employ it as a weapon against the powerful (as per Friedrich Nietzsche[72]), often in a counterattack against the misuse of the Bible by the powerful. When we pick up the Bible, we want to know who has done what mischief to whom in and with these texts. As masters of our own destinies averse to all power-ploys, we sense in the Bible a danger to ourselves and to others.

One way to eliminate the danger is to read the Bible by systematically employing a "hermeneutic of suspicion." Except for the people whose lives are claimed by fundamentalist religious communities — the people who have a hard time warding off the assault undertaken with the weapon called "the Bible" — in an age of individual choices and shifting commitments suspicion is easy and its thrills are cheap. The main lesson we learn from the three great masters of suspicion — Karl Marx, Friedrich Nietzsche, and Sigmund Freud — is not so much to be suspicious. Instead, we learn how easy it is for gifted and imaginative minds to interpret any text, indeed a whole centuries-long tradition, as expressing some underlying base attitudes and covering up ugly practices. After all, the three of them cannot all be correct, for the main thrusts of their readings are incompatible yet each offers a compelling, subversive, overarching reading of the Bible!

From the masters of suspicion we also learn how seductive a herme-

71. Karl Marx, *Critique of Hegel's 'Philosophy of Right'* (ed. and introduction by Joseph O'Malley; trans. Annette Jolin and Joseph O'Malley; Cambridge: Cambridge University Press, 1970).

72. Friedrich Nietzsche, *Genealogy of Morals: A Polemic* (trans. Horace B. Samuel; New York: Macmillan, 1924).

neutic of suspicion can be. As we watch them at work, we feel the excitement of voyeurs, observing as one after another layer of protective clothing is stripped away from a cherished tradition, until all we see is the "naked truth" — the ugly truth of exposed hypocrisy, in this case. As a comprehensive approach to the Bible, the hermeneutic of suspicion is not a method of interpretation, it is a strategy for "debunking."[73] We employ it and then, as Marx, Nietzsche, and Freud did, walk away from what has turned out to be an untruthful and harmful rather than insightful and salutary book, a base text rather than a genuinely sacred one.

Approaching the Bible as a genuinely sacred text calls for a *hermeneutic of respect* rather than a hermeneutic of suspicion.[74] We approach it with an attitude of receptivity appropriate to the presumption — maybe always only a provisional presumption — that it is a site of God's self-revelation. We read it expecting that by finding ourselves and our world in the story of God's dealings with humanity, we will (re)discover our true identities and the world's proper destiny. We study it anticipating that we will discover the wisdom to help individuals, communities, and our entire planet genuinely to flourish. We read it trusting that we will learn better to love God and neighbor.

But should we not mistrust the proposed hermeneutic of respect? It seems to undermine critical judgment and leave us in an excessively passive relation to the text. Yet this need not be the case. First, "respect" and "receptivity" are not incompatible with critical judgment; instead, critical judgment ought to accompany them. True, many who are committed to something like a hermeneutic of respect are tempted, as Job's comforters were, to "speak falsely for God" in order to defend the trustworthiness of the Bible.[75] But neither God nor God's Word needs such defenders. Indeed, Job's point is that they dishonor God. It will not go well with them, he states, when the God of truth and justice "searches them out" (Job 13:7-12; 42:7-9).

73. For how a hermeneutic of suspicion and project of unmasking fits larger cultural trends, see Russell R. Reno, "The Antinomian Threat to Human Flourishing" (unpublished manuscript).

74. On respect as the proper stance toward the Bible as the Holy Scripture see David Kelsey, *Eccentric Existence*, 140-56.

75. See Collins, "Biblical Theology," 21.

But many of us are not instinctively defenders of the Bible. Its world strikes us as strange, and as we walk around in it we sometimes come across what seems to us to be an absence of sense. If we practice a hermeneutic of respect, however, we can continue to engage the text without suppressing puzzlement or even negative judgment, while patiently waiting for the sense to emerge, either as a result of a new insight or of a personal transformation. In our encounter with the Bible, tarrying in persistent non-understanding is often the condition of the possibility of genuine disclosure, in which we hear more than just the echo of our own internal voice.[76]

It is possible that no disclosure will arrive, and that what we deem "non-sense" — moral or otherwise — will continue stubbornly to stare at us from the pages of the sacred book. The command that Israel blot out the memory of Amalek from under heaven by killing all the descendants of those who hindered Israel on its journey to the Promised Land (Deuteronomy 25:19) may never yield sense to us within the context of the larger narrative of the Bible. Similarly, even after giving the apostle Paul the benefit of the doubt, it may remain unacceptable to us that he would describe "the Jews" as hostile to all people (1 Thessalonians 2:14-15). In cases of these and other "texts of terror,"[77] we have two limiting options that define the parameters of our compelling choices. We can give up on the Bible and, with it, on Christian theology and Christian faith. Or, if we find Christian faith too compelling to reject, we can wrestle with and try to gain insight from the uncomfortable, paradoxical "non-sense" that stands right in the midst of the sacred text through which we make sense of everything.[78]

76. On the importance of *non-understanding* for encounter with the other, see Volf, *Exclusion and Embrace*, 143-44.

77. "Texts of terror" is the famous phrase of Phyllis Trible (*Texts of Terror: Literary-Feminist Readings of Biblical Narratives* [Philadelphia: Fortress, 1984]).

78. In sketching these two limiting options, I am assuming that the Bible offers and Christian faith entails an overarching perspective on life rather than a few nuggets of wisdom or a view about a particular aspect — called "religions," maybe — of human life. Not all Christians view the Bible and their faith in this way, especially not today in an age of smorgasbord religiosity and hybridized religious identities. But it is how I view the Christian faith, and it is how the great Christian theologians and compelling Christian saints have viewed it over the centuries. If my assumption about the Bible and the

Second, though they may seem like passive qualities, "respect" and "receptivity" are compatible with bringing ourselves — and our communities — into the reading process. To receive anything is an *action*, as any catcher of a ball thrown her way will attest. To receive well in reading the Bible, I must not only receive actively, but I must also receive *as myself*. At the receiving end of the reading process is a person living at a particular time and place as part of a particular community, not a generic member of the human race; a person with a particular history and shaped by a determinate set of influences; a human being dreaming particular dreams and plagued by particular fears, driven by specific aversions and energized by particular loves. I never read the Bible as an abstract human being (there are no abstract human beings!), though as a concrete human being I may well read it with a view of what it says about every human being or about all human beings together. But I always read the Bible as myself. Indeed, the more I am consciously present as myself in the act of reading, the more profitable the reading is likely to be. And, inversely, the more I profit from the sacred text that tells my story within the story of God's dealings with the world, the more I will truly be myself.[79]

The active presence of the concrete self in receptivity, which properly characterizes the reading of the Bible, loops back to the historicality of the Bible itself (and to the closely related multiplicity of its meanings). It is the subjective side of God's involvement in the lives of people. Both

---

Christian faith is correct, then by definition nothing is external to that perspective; everything is viewed through that particular lens. Of course, I can imaginatively inhabit other overarching perspectives on life, learn a very great deal indeed from sources other than the Bible, and integrate that learning in one way or another into my overarching perspective; not *all* the gold of the Egyptians need be melted! Alternatively, I can also come to the point of asserting that the overarching Christian perspective is incoherent and uninhabitable and that therefore it must be abandoned. But the way I see things, I must always choose *an* overarching perspective (or default to one) from which to view everything.

79. It would be a mistake to feel forced to choose between "humble receptivity" and "imaginative engagement" in the reading of the Scripture. If I read *as myself*, I will read employing imagination; but since I am reading a sacred text, a site of God's self-revelation (rather than, say, merely a deposit of ancient nuggets of religious wisdom that I may use in my own spiritual quest by incorporating them into my own ever-changing spiritual profile), the employment of imagination can be a mode of receptivity.

of these closely related phenomena are signaled in the description of the event that marked the birth of the Church — the coming of the Holy Spirit on the disciples gathered after Christ's resurrection and ascension. By the power of the Spirit, their first act as a newborn Church was to speak in the native languages of many peoples. The disciples witnessed to "God's deeds of power" (Acts 2:11), but did so in ways that were suitable to the varied modes of receptivity of the actual people present. The one message for all people was translated into many languages of different peoples, so that all could receive it *as themselves*.[80]

The Christian Scriptures and Other Faiths

I have argued that the Bible is a book for today; it is the Holy Scripture of Christian communities. But do you need to be a Christian, acculturated to Christian ways of thinking, speaking, and acting, to read it with profit? Do you need to be a Christian theologian to read it theologically? Can people of other faiths, or of no traditional faith, benefit from reading the Bible?

They do — and therefore they can.[81] For instance, a few years ago on the television program "Genesis: A Living Conversation," Bill Moyers spoke to people from various walks of life, embracing diverse faiths, about the great issues addressed in the first book of the Bible. Conversation topics ranged "from the creation of the world to its destruction by flood, from the first man and woman made in God's image to the intrigues of the patriarchs and matriarchs, from fratricide to reconciliation, from being called by God to calling on God."[82] Despite the wide range of backgrounds and perspectives, a conversation was not only pos-

80. On the importance of translation, see Lamin Sanneh, *Translating the Message: The Missionary Impact on Culture* (Maryknoll, N.Y.: Orbis, 1989).

81. David Ford, one of the most prominent theological readers of Scripture, suggests the following as one of his maxims for reading the Bible: "Let conversation around scripture be open to all people, religions, cultures, arts, disciplines, media and spheres of life" (Ford, *Christian Wisdom*, 87).

82. Cf. Bill Moyers, "Genesis — A Living Conversation," PBS, http://www.pbs.org/wnet/genesis/program.html.

sible, but was deeply meaningful and even arresting. To take another example from a very different setting, when non-Christian college students with no background in religious studies read the first pages of the Bible under the guidance of an atheist professor they can clearly identify the deep questions of life it addresses and connect them with their own quests for truth and meaning.[83]

An impressive testimony to the fruitfulness of the Christian Bible in conversations among people of different faiths is the Scriptural Reasoning Project. Its "philosophy" is simple, even if it takes careful and sophisticated intellectual work to describe it adequately. When Jews, Christians, and Muslims meet together for interfaith exchanges, they should not leave aside their particularities as religious people and speak to each other as generic human beings. Instead, the group asserts, they should plunge into the dialogue as Jews, Christians, and Muslims, and take their respective scriptures as their "primary focus."[84] At the center of their mutual interfaith engagement should be the practice of reading together each other's scriptures. The privileging of scripture may seem counterintuitive. After all, since each tradition's scripture is the primary source of its identity, one might expect that engagement with each other's scriptures would result in an unproductive clash of identities. In the case of Christians and Muslims, it might be a face-off between interlocutors who say, "This-is-what-I-think-and-who-I-am-because-this-is-what-the-Bible-says" vs. "This-is-what-I-think-and-who-I-am-because-this-is-what-the-Qur'an-says."

Yet often the very opposite takes place. Even the most devout — maybe *especially* the most devout — followers of a faith find the engagement with the scriptures of another faith both fascinating and generative. As participants alternate in inhabiting the world of each other's scriptures, two things tend to happen. First, we learn to understand others better (because we listen to how others interpret their own identity-

83. Anthony Kronman, Sterling Professor of Law at Yale University, in a conversation on the topic of teaching Genesis as part of "Directed Studies."

84. David Ford, "An Interfaith Wisdom: Scriptural Reasoning between Jews, Christians, and Muslims," chap. 1 in *The Promise of Scriptural Reasoning* (ed. David F. Ford and C. C. Pecknold; Oxford: Wiley-Blackwell, 2007). See also the literature cited in footnote 28 (above).

shaping texts), and they come to understand themselves better (because they see themselves and their own scriptures through eyes of others). Second, listening to how one's own scriptures are interpreted by others, as well as interpreting one's own scriptures in the presence of others, often brings to life disregarded or backgrounded aspects of one's tradition. As a consequence, we not only understand our tradition better, but we begin to formulate it (partly) differently. Almost without exception, reading each other's scriptures is illuminating and generative for all involved. With scriptures at the center of engagement, the identity of each participant is secured because it is tied to her or his own sacred text; and *because* of that, each person can embark upon a mutually transformative journey with people of different faiths.

Granted, in such interfaith encounters sacred books will not have the same status for all participants. The holy book of my religious community is, obviously, sacred to me — in the case of Muslims and Christians, for instance, scripture is the Word of God. I also recognize that your holy book is sacred to you. But my holy book will not be sacred to you or yours to me, at least not in the same sense. But for us to read our sacred books fruitfully together, they do not need to be holy to both of us. It suffices that each treats the holy book of the other as a classic spiritual text. People with differing overarching interpretations of life can engage each other with openness and argumentative rigor at the place where the river of "classic" meats the sea of "sacred." As people encounter each other in this estuary,[85] their lives will acquire richness and depth.

Conclusion

These, then, are my interpretive commitments. I read the Bible as a sacred text and a witness to Jesus Christ; a site of God's self-revelation; a text from the past through which God addresses all humanity and each human being today; a text that has an overarching unity yet is internally teeming with rich diversity; a text that encodes meanings and refracts

---

85. I owe the image of estuary as a place of encounter for diverse cultures to my friend and artist Makoto Fujimora.

them in multiple ways; a text we should approach with trust and critical judgment as well as engage with receptivity and imagination; a text that defines Christian identity yet speaks to people beyond the boundaries of Christian communities. Whether discussing St. Peter's reflections on Christians as "aliens and sojourners" (chapter 3) or Ecclesiastes' warnings about the futility of human striving (chapter 6), whether engaging St. John's oppositional dualities of "light and darkness" (chapter 4) or his claim that "God is love" (chapter 5), or whether learning from St. Paul's ways of doing theology (chapter 2), these convictions comprise the framework in which I read the Bible, the lens through which I am interpreting it. As I, in my own fashion, have joined theologians of the past in sipping from the well of Scripture, theological readings of the Bible have helped me form a vision of life that is lived lovingly before God and joyfully with neighbor. I hope that these essays will serve as an invitation to others to come and drink from that same inexhaustible well which is Scripture, the site of God's self-revelation for the sake of humanity's integral salvation.

CHAPTER TWO

Theology for a Way of Life

The Challenge of "Real" Life

"But what does that have to do with *real* life?" I have come to expect an occasional question like this one in courses on systematic theology. So if students complain that theology is too "theoretical," I invite them to consider Kant's argument that nothing is as practical as a good theory.[1] If they object that theologians entertain outdated and therefore irrelevant ideas, I offer them a Kierkegaardian observation that the right kind of noncontemporaneity may be more timely than today's newspaper. I conclude by explaining how ideas that seem detached from everyday concerns may in fact touch the very heart of those concerns.

And yet, when I am done with my disquisition, I have dealt with only half the worry expressed in my students' skeptical questions. We theologians sometimes do teach and write as though we have made a studied effort to avoid contact with the "impurities" of human lives. We do so

---

1. Immanuel Kant, "On the Common Saying: 'This May Be True in Theory, but It Does Not Apply in Practice,'" in *Kant: Political Writings* (ed. Hans Reiss; trans. H. B. Nisbet; 2d ed.; Cambridge/New York: Cambridge University Press, 1991), 61.

This paper originally appeared in *Practicing Theology,* edited by Miroslav Volf and Dorothy C. Bass (Grand Rapids: Eerdmans, 2002).

partly by our choice of topics. The number of pages theologians have devoted to the question of transubstantiation — which does or does not take place on any given Sunday — would, I suspect, far exceed the number of pages we have devoted to the daily work that fills our lives Monday through Saturday. We also take flight from the concerns of the quotidian by how we treat great theological themes such as the Trinity, Christology, and soteriology. As thinkers we rightly focus on conceptual difficulties — "How can God be one and three persons at the same time?" "How can Christ be both God and man?" "How can we owe salvation to nothing but grace and yet be free?" — but in the process we sometimes lose the larger significance of these doctrines. Moreover, as academics we are caught in the movement toward increased specialization. On the one hand, specialization seems a necessary condition for fundamental research. On the other hand, it tends to make us lose sight of the overarching subject of theology. The scholarly interests of theologians then fail to match the realities of the people in the pew and on the street.[2]

There is yet another important reason for a perceived disconnect between theology and so-called "real" life. It lies in the distinction between the theoretical and the practical sciences that goes all the way back to Aristotle and his disciples. According to this distinction, the goal of the theoretical sciences is truth, and the goal of the practical sciences is action. Aristotle considered the theoretical sciences, in which knowledge is pursued for knowledge's sake, a higher wisdom than the practical sciences, which are pursued for their usefulness.[3] It has long been debated how theology fits into this Aristotelian scheme. Thomas Aquinas, for instance, weighed in on the side of theology being a theoretical science,[4] and Duns Scotus argued it was a practical one.[5] Obviously, if theology is a theoretical science, then it only secondarily has something to do with practices; one has to make separate inquiry into the practical implications of knowledge pursued for its own sake. But if theology is a

---

2. See Miroslav Volf, "Introduction: A Queen and a Beggar: Challenges and Prospects of Theology," in *The Future of Theology: Essays in Honor of Jürgen Moltmann* (ed. Miroslav Volf et al.; Grand Rapids: Eerdmans, 1996), ix-xviii.

3. See Aristotle, *Metaphysics,* 982a 14ff. and 993b 20-21.

4. Thomas Aquinas, *Summa Theologiae* I.1.4.

5. Duns Scotus, *Ordinatio,* prol. pars 5, qq. 1-2.

practical science, then practices are from the start included within the purview of its concerns.

Often theologians have done theology as though it were a theoretical science; this, too, has contributed to a sense that theology is unrelated to "real" life. In different ways, the essays in this volume all share the persuasion that theology is more properly described as a practical than as a theoretical science — "science" in the loose sense of critical and methodologically disciplined reflection.[6] Here I will explore in more general terms how we should understand this claim. I will argue that theology is an (academic) enterprise whose object of study is God and God's relation to the world and whose purpose is not simply to deliver "knowledge," but to serve a way of life. Put slightly differently, my contention is that *at the heart of every good theology lies not simply a plausible intellectual vision but more importantly a compelling account of a way of life, and that theology is therefore best done from within the pursuit of this way of life.* I will begin with a story that revolves around a practice, then reflect on its implications for the relation between beliefs and practices and therefore also for the relation between systematic theology (as a critical reflection on beliefs) and a way of life (as the sum of Christian practices).

Before I proceed, I should briefly indicate what I mean by "beliefs" and "practices." First, I am using the term "beliefs" in the sense of the "core Christian beliefs." In the life of individuals these are convictions implicit in the basic act of faith, through which God constitutes human beings as Christians; they are the ideational side of the most basic act of faith.[7] In the life of Christian communities, core beliefs are convictions

6. I am leaving aside here the question of whether or to what extent theology is a science in the same sense as other sciences. On this question, see Wolfhart Pannenberg, *Theology and the Philosophy of Science* (trans. F. McDonagh; Philadelphia: Westminster, 1976), 23-224; Philip Clayton, *Explanation from Physics to Theology: An Essay in Rationality and Religion* (New Haven: Yale University Press, 1989), 154-67; Nancey Murphy, *Theology in the Age of Scientific Reasoning* (Ithaca, N.Y.: Cornell University Press, 1990), 174-208; Wentzel van Huyssteen, *The Shaping of Rationality: Toward Interdisciplinarity in Theology and Science* (Grand Rapids: Eerdmans, 1999).

7. My "core beliefs" overlap in significant ways with the notion of "doctrine" that Reinhard Hütter employs in "Hospitality and Truth: The Disclosure of Practices in Worship and Doctrine," in *Practicing Theology: Beliefs and Practices in Christian Life* (ed. Miroslav Volf and Dorothy C. Bass; Grand Rapids: Eerdmans, 2002), 206-27. See also

that a Christian community "must hold true in order to maintain its own identity."[8] "Beliefs," in my usage here, is equivalent to "authentic doctrines."

Second, I am using the term "practices" in the sense of cooperative and meaningful human endeavors that seek to satisfy fundamental human needs and conditions and that people do together and over time.[9] With this brief statement I could be done with describing my use of practices were it not that a relation between practices and sacraments features prominently in my text. Sacraments can be plausibly construed as practices, but I use "practices" in a narrower sense that does not include sacraments, for no other reason than to keep historically situated and cooperative activities that satisfy fundamental human needs ("practices") conceptually distinct from sacraments. The distinction is especially important to maintain in treatments of the relation between beliefs and practices, because beliefs — I am running a little ahead of myself here — relate to sacraments differently from the way they relate to "practices." Core Christian beliefs are *by definition normatively inscribed in sacraments* but not in "practices." Hence sacraments ritually enact normative patterns for practices.

Strangers and Hosts

His name I have forgotten, but the image of him at our table is indelible. On the first Sunday of every month he would make his way from the back country to the city of Novi Sad in Yugoslavia, where my father was pastor of a small Pentecostal church. Our guest, the lone Pentecostal in his village, who was surrounded by a sea of hostile nonbelievers and Orthodox Christians, would come to our church for Holy Communion. After feasting at the Lord's Table, he would join our family for the Sunday meal. A

Hütter's notion of "doctrina evangelii" in *Suffering Divine Things: Theology as Church Practice* (trans. Doug Stott; Grand Rapids: Eerdmans, 2000), 135-45.

8. Bruce D. Marshall, *Trinity and Truth* (Cambridge: Cambridge University Press, 2000), 19.

9. See Craig Dykstra and Dorothy C. Bass's definition in "A Theological Understanding of Christian Practices," in Volf and Bass, eds., *Practicing Theology,* 18.

rough-hewn figure, both intriguing and slightly menacing, he would sit quietly, a bit hunched, at the table opposite me, a teenage boy. A moustache that put Nietzsche's to shame dominated his face.

I resented his coming, for when he entered our house my memory would always play back a sound from his previous visit. The sound was that of my mother's soup — delicious to the point that whatever preceded and followed it served only to frame its unsurpassable taste — leaping noisily across the gap between his spoon and his mouth through his moustache. And so the climax of the week's menu, as Mary Douglas calls the Sunday lunch,[10] was ruined for me. Though my parents never said anything, I could sense their unease with our visitor's manners. Yet they not only thought it important to invite him repeatedly, but also admired the robustness of his commitment despite the great adversity he suffered on account of his faith.

One could apply a hermeneutic of suspicion to my parents' practice. They wanted to impress parishioners, atone for secret guilt, make payments into a heavenly investment portfolio. In their own minds, however, they were extending the invitation to this stranger because they did not think one should hold the table of the Lord at which my father presided in the morning apart from the table of our home at whose head he was sitting at noon. I am not sure how much they *knew* about the original unity of the eucharistic celebration and the agape meal, but they clearly *practiced* their inseparability. Had I objected — "But must *we* invite him *every* time he comes!?" — they would have responded, "As the Lord gave his body and blood for us sinners, so we ought to be ready to share with strangers not only our belongings but also something of our very selves." The circle of our table was opened by the wounds of Christ, and a stranger was let in. Had I continued to protest, they would have reminded me of that grand eschatological meal whose host will be the Triune God, a meal at which people of every tribe and tongue will be feasting. I had better be ready to sit next to him at *that* meal, they would have insisted.

The relation between the ecclesial and eschatological table and the

10. Mary Douglas, "Deciphering a Meal," in *Myth, Symbol, and Culture* (ed. Clifford Geertz; New York: W. W. Norton & Co., 1971), 67.

many tables to which we do or do not invite guests is a case in point of the relation between beliefs — some of them ritually enacted — and practices. The sacrament of the Lord's Supper itself is very much a summary of the whole of Christian life, at whose heart lies the self-giving of God for sinful humanity,[11] and the eschatological Feast is the sum of Christian hopes for communion between the Triune God and God's glorified people. So how do some of the most basic and sacramentally enacted Christian convictions intersect with the practice of hospitality?

Belief-shaped Practices

At one level, the answer to the question of how Christian beliefs and practices intersect seems plain enough — if my parents' practice offers a window on the way beliefs relate to practices. The celebration of the Lord's Supper, and a whole range of beliefs that are embedded in it and that explain why and how it is undertaken, shaped my parents' practice of hospitality. So Christian beliefs shape Christian practices. But how, more precisely? One can explore how beliefs shape practices from two angles: by examining the nature of Christian practices, and the nature of Christian beliefs.

Let us look first at the issue from the angle of practices. Christian practices have what we may call an "as-so" structure (or correspondence structure): *as* God has received us in Christ, *so* we too are to receive our fellow human beings. True, the way in which Christ's life is exemplary has to be carefully specified. Above all, the important difference between Christ and other human beings should counter both the temptation to supplant Christ and the presumption that human beings can simply "repeat" Christ's work. But in an appropriately qualified way, in relation to the practice of hospitality as well as in relation to all other practices, we must say: "As Christ, so we."[12]

11. See the brief reflections on Eucharist as "ordering ritual" in Ingolf U. Dalferth, *Theology and Philosophy* (Oxford: Blackwell, 1988), 222-23.

12. For an extended exemplification of the "as-so" structure of Christian practices, see Miroslav Volf, *Exclusion and Embrace: Theological Reflections on Identity, Otherness, and Reconciliation* (Nashville: Abingdon, 1996).

Beliefs about who Christ is and what Christ did, expressed in the form of narratives, ritual actions, or propositions, provide the norm for the Christian practice of hospitality. This practice is Christian only insofar as Christ serves as the model for its practitioners, and Christ is available as a model only through such beliefs. This is not to say that practices of non-Christians cannot be Christomorphic; they often are. But to be a Christian *is* to believe explicitly in Christ and commit oneself to follow his way of life. Thus the internal constitution of a *Christian* practice points to the story of Christ as its external norm. Hospitality as a Christian practice is suffused with particular Christian beliefs that shape it normatively. Put more generally, Christian practices are *by definition* normatively shaped by Christian beliefs.

Our guests have gone home. As we clean the dishes, we muse about whether we have been good hosts. We ask ourselves many different questions, but if we are engaged in Christian hospitality we will examine what we did in the light of the story of Christ, in the light of his words and deeds. We will, for instance, remember the following injunction from the third Gospel:

> When you give a luncheon or a dinner, do not invite your friends or your brothers or your relatives or rich neighbors, in case they may invite you in return, and you would be repaid. But when you give a banquet, invite the poor, the crippled, the lame, and the blind. And you will be blessed, because they cannot repay you, for you will be repaid at the resurrection of the righteous. (Luke 14:12-14)

From this we may conclude that hospitality at its best should not be part of the economy of exchange among equals or with superiors, but instead be part of an economy of donation to the destitute and weak. So to evaluate whether we were good hosts, we might ask ourselves whether we expected to get as much (or more) out of the invitation as we put in. If we did, we have missed the mark.

There is a second way in which Christian practices are unthinkable without Christian beliefs. The story of Christ, which informs the "as-so" pattern, is itself embedded in the larger story of God with Israel and the nations, and this larger story again is framed by the narratives of God's

47

creation and final consummation. That nexus of stories draws a map of the normative space in which human beings exist as agents of Christian practices. As Charles Taylor has argued in *Sources of the Self,* such a space is essential for moral action because it is within it that "questions arise about what is good or bad, what is worth doing and what is not, what has meaning and importance for you and what is trivial and secondary."[13] Christian beliefs are indispensable for the creation of the Christian moral space in which alone engagement in Christian practices makes sense.

Practice-shaping Beliefs

By attending to the character of Christian practices, we have observed an intimate link between beliefs and practices. We see a similar link when we consider the nature of Christian beliefs. Shaping practices — shaping a way of life — is internal to the very nature of these beliefs.

To determine whether beliefs are essentially practice-shaping, it is particularly important to examine the nature of beliefs about God. These beliefs lie at the heart of the Christian faith, and the tradition has therefore rightly claimed that God and God's relation to the world constitute the proper "object" of theology.[14] Everything theology studies is studied, as Wolfhart Pannenberg states in *Theology and the Philosophy of Science,* "from the point of view of its relation to God *(sub ratione Dei).* It is only this consideration *sub ratione Dei* which distinguishes the treatment of a wide range of topics in theology from their treatment in other disciplines which concern themselves with the same areas but from different points of view."[15] Because beliefs about God shape the whole of theology, the relation of these beliefs to practices is at the heart of the issue we are discussing.

---

13. Charles Taylor, *Sources of the Self: The Making of the Modern Identity* (Cambridge, Mass.: Harvard University Press, 1989), 28.

14. For different accounts of theological enterprise which are agreed on the basic idea that God is the subject of theology see, for instance, Pannenberg, *Theology and the Philosophy of Science,* and David Kelsey, *To Understand God Truly: What's Theological about a Theological School* (Louisville: Westminster John Knox, 1992).

15. Pannenberg, *Theology and the Philosophy of Science,* 298.

Consider one important feature of beliefs about God. It emerges as soon as one remembers that God is not an object in the world to which human beings may or may not be related in significant ways. Rather, God is the creator, redeemer, and consummator of all that is. Human beings live in a relation of inescapable dependence on God — dependence that grounds human freedom along with all other human good and is in no way incompatible with it[16] — to which gratitude is the appropriate response. Moreover, the identity of human beings and the goal of their lives are bound up with the fact that God created them to image God and live in communion with God. The "as-so" structure, which we noted in how what Christ did for sinful humanity relates to our practices ("as Christ, so we"), applies more generally to the relation between who God is and who human beings are and therefore how they ought to behave ("as God, so we").

This claim is *already implied* in the affirmation of God's existence — which is to say, in the affirmation that a relationship between God and human beings obtains such that human beings owe their existence to God and find their fulfillment in imaging God and living in communion with God. As a consequence, whenever we speak of God, we are always involved; the import of the claims about God for human beings does not need to be brought in subsequently but is already part and parcel of the talk about God. As Gerhard Ebeling puts it in commenting on the way Luther speaks of God, "what is said of God does not have to be applied later to man . . . what is said of God is addressed to man."[17]

What bearing does this claim about the nature of Christian beliefs have on the relation between beliefs and practices? Rightly to espouse the belief that God is "the God of peace" (Rom. 15:33), for instance, *is*, among other things, to commit oneself to the pursuit of peace. Similarly, the obligation to ensure that one person does not "go hungry" while "another becomes drunk" is part and parcel of believing rightly about the

16. See Karl Rahner, *Foundations of Christian Faith* (trans. W. Dych; New York: Crossroad, 1978), 79; Kathryn Tanner, *Jesus, Humanity, and the Trinity: A Brief Systematic Theology* (Minneapolis: Fortress, 2001), 2-4.

17. Gerhard Ebeling, *Luther: An Introduction to His Thought* (trans. R. A. Wilson; Philadelphia: Fortress, 1972), 248. See also Gerhard Ebeling, "Cognitio Dei et hominis," in *Lutherstudien* (vol. 1; Tübingen: Mohr, 1971), 221-72.

Lord's Supper (1 Cor. 11:21). No doubt one can believe and fail to act accordingly; one can believe and expressly intend not to act accordingly.[18] Indeed, as the Old Testament prophets' critique of religious devotion makes manifest, one can profess a belief precisely in order not to act accordingly.[19] But such situations are clearly at odds with the inner dynamics of beliefs themselves — otherwise one could not cover one's wrongdoing with a demonstrative profession of belief. Espousing a belief puts pressure on the one who believes to act accordingly. Put more generally, basic Christian beliefs *as beliefs* entail practical commitments. These commitments may need to be explicated so as to become clear, or they may need to be connected to specific issues in concrete situations, but they do not need to be *added* to the beliefs; they inhere in the beliefs. Christian beliefs are not simply statements about what was, is, and will be the case; they are statements about what *should* be the case and what human beings should do about that.[20] They provide a normative vision for practices.

To sum up my argument thus far: Christian practices are such that a Christian normative vision is part and parcel of what these practices are; and Christian beliefs are such that informing Christian practices is part and parcel of what these beliefs do. Practices are essentially belief-shaped, and beliefs are essentially practice-shaping.

Grace, Beliefs, Practices

The role of beliefs in relation to practices is not only providing a normative vision for practices; from a theological standpoint, this role of be-

---

18. For an analysis of disconnects between beliefs and practices see Amy Plantinga Pauw, "Attending to the Gaps between Beliefs and Practices," in Volf and Bass, eds., *Practicing Theology*, 33-48.

19. See Miroslav Volf, *Zukunft der Arbeit — Arbeit der Zukunft. Das Marxsche Arbeitsverständnis und seine theologische Wertung* (Munich: Kaiser, 1988), 106; Hans-Joachim Kraus, *Theologische Religionskritik* (Neukirchen-Vluyn: Neukirchener Verlag, 1982), 251.

20. See Jürgen Moltmann, *Theology of Hope: On the Ground and the Implications of a Christian Eschatology* (trans. J. W. Leitch; London: SCM, 1967).

liefs, though immensely important, is secondary. The whole Christian way of life, with all its practices, is supported and shaped by something outside that way of life — by what God has done, is doing, and will do. The Christian faith is not primarily about human doing; the gospel is not reducible to the barebones formal injunction, "Look at Christ and imitate a wholesome way of life," or "Understand God and act accordingly." The Christian faith is not primarily about human *doing* but about human *receiving*. The barebones formal injunction to which the gospel can be reduced is, "Receive yourself and your world as a new creation." More than just normatively guiding practices, Christian beliefs narrate the divine action by which human beings are constituted as agents of practices, by which they are placed into a determinate normative space, and by which they are inspired and charged to imitate God.[21]

Consider once again the Lord's Supper. Eating the bread and drinking the wine, we remember the body broken for God's enemies and the blood spilled to establish a "new covenant" with those who have broken the covenant. In that act of ritual commemoration we dramatize the central elements of a normative vision that should guide our practices. But if that were all we thought we were doing, we would be profoundly misunderstanding the Lord's Supper. Central to the celebration of the Lord's Supper is the truth that the body was broken and the blood spilled "for us" and for the "life of the world." The Lord's Supper is a sacramental re-presentation of the gift of new life through Christ's death and resurrection — new life, whose reality underlies every single properly Christian act and therefore all Christian practices. Understandings of how the gift of new life is re-presented in the Lord's Supper differ, but most agree about the primacy of the eucharistic reference to the divine work for us, rather than our imitation of that work.

Of course, we would also be misunderstanding the Lord's Supper if we thought of it only as a sacrament of God's embrace, of which we are simply the fortunate beneficiaries. Inscribed in the very heart of God's grace is the rule that we can be its recipients only if we do not resist being made into its agents. In a precisely defined way that guards the dis-

---

21. On the constitution of the Christian subject see Karl Barth, *Church Dogmatics* (ed. G. W. Bromiley and T. F. Torrance; Edinburgh: T. & T. Clark, 1957-67), IV/1, 749.

tinction between God and human beings, human beings themselves are made participants in the divine activity and therefore are inspired, empowered, and obliged to imitate it. Which is where practices come in.[22] Christian practices may be construed as human "resonances,"[23] under a variety of circumstances, of the divine engagement with the world through which human beings are sustained and redeemed.

First Come Practices

My argument so far about the relation between beliefs and practices amounts to the claim that Christian beliefs do not express "pure knowledge" but are intended to guide Christian practices by situating the practitioner within the overarching narrative of God's dealings with humanity and by offering an account of his or her constitution as an agent. Seen from within that way of life, beliefs describe the constitution of agents of practices and offer normative direction for that way of life. So beliefs shape practices. But do practices contribute anything to beliefs?

One way to explore this issue is to ask the following question: Do we first accept Christian beliefs and then engage in Christian practices, or the other way around? As attested by the accounts of those who have experienced conversion through reading the Bible without having had previous contact with Christians, one can accept Christian beliefs without previously engaging in Christian practices or even observing Christian practices. A person can start engaging in Christian practices because he or she has found Christian beliefs intellectually compelling. In such cases, Christian beliefs come first and Christian practices follow.

As a rule, however, this is not how things happen. People come to believe either because they find themselves already engaged in Christian practices (say, by being raised in a Christian home) or because they are attracted to them. In most cases, Christian practices come first and Chris-

22. In "A Theological Understanding of Christian Practices," Dorothy Bass and Craig Dykstra have underscored that Christian practices are forms of participation in divine activity.

23. For a theological appropriation of the notion of "resonances," see Michael Welker, *God the Spirit* (trans. John F. Hoffmeyer; Minneapolis: Fortress, 1994), 313ff.

tian beliefs follow — or rather, beliefs are already entailed in practices, so that their explicit espousing becomes a matter of bringing to consciousness what is implicit in the engagement in practices themselves.

Recall my parents' example. Notwithstanding my occasional grumbling at the liberality with which my parents practiced hospitality toward people around whom I felt uneasy, I arguably have embraced the Christian faith along with its core beliefs partly because I saw it embodied in their practices. Moreover, the way they engaged in the practice of hospitality profoundly shaped the way I came to understand basic Christian beliefs (just as the way my saintly nanny treated me as a young boy helped form my image of God). People make Christian beliefs their own and understand them in particular ways partly because of the practices to which they have been introduced — in which their souls and bodies have been trained[24] — in the course of their lives. Put differently, by being attracted to and habituated in a set of practices, they have embraced the set of beliefs that sustain these practices and that are inscribed in them.

The movement from practices to beliefs is, however, not as simple as my account so far suggests. It is not at all clear that I would have *rejected* the Christian faith had I seen a major discrepancy between my parents' beliefs and practices. What if I had overheard them say to each other the evening after we had entertained our guest, "What a brute! He will never step into our house again," and if from that day on we had invited to our table only those who "behaved"? It does not follow that I would have concluded either that the Lord's Supper was just a religious sham or that, my soul and body not having been trained in the practice of inviting strangers, the Lord's Supper does not contain an imperative to do so. Instead, I might simply have deemed my parents weak, inconsistent, or even hypocritical, and embraced the beliefs they espoused and ritually celebrated with a determination to live a more consistent life (much in the way a person might respond internally to an animal-rights activist who eats meat).

On the other hand, even the excellence of my parents' Christian practices need not have led to my espousal of Christian beliefs. In fact, at

24. On the socially informed body, see Pierre Bourdieu, *Outline of a Theory of Practice* (trans. R. Nice; Cambridge: Cambridge University Press, 1977), 124.

one point in my life, the exact opposite happened. I rejected the faith precisely because my parents were such good practitioners and because their practices had held a claim on my life. The dissonance between the practices of the peer group with which I identified and my parents' practices, and the clash between what I was taught at school (Marxist indoctrination!) and some basic Christian beliefs, were simply too great. In my teenage years, my parents seemed to me to be duped and dense people who were imposing on me an outdated way of life. When it comes to embracing or rejecting Christian beliefs, practices do influence beliefs, but they do so in complex and not always predictable ways.

The second way in which practices are crucial for beliefs concerns not so much the acceptance of beliefs but their *understanding*. What George Lindbeck says in *The Nature of Doctrine* about proclamation is true of all Christian belief: "[it] gains power and meaning insofar as it is embodied in the total gestalt of community life and action."[25] "Right (communal) doing" seems in some sense a precondition for right understanding. The obverse is also true: "wrong doing" — especially if deeply patterned and long lived — leads to twisted understanding. It would be, however, too much to claim that the "wrong-doers" *cannot* know rightly and that the "right-doers" *cannot* know wrongly. The connection between engaging practices and understanding beliefs is a loose one. Nonetheless, right practices well practiced *are likely to* open persons for insights into beliefs to which they would otherwise be closed.[26] Inversely, wrong practices can "suppress the truth" (Rom. 1:18), that is, have an adverse impact on which beliefs are deemed true and how beliefs that are deemed true are understood.

For theology, the hermeneutical impact of practices is crucial for the simple reason that the formulation of Christian beliefs is fundamentally a hermeneutical task. So far I have spoken only of "core beliefs" or "authentic doctrines." But we always hold these core beliefs in situationally rendered forms. Such rendering is done implicitly and explicitly simply

25. George A. Lindbeck, *The Nature of Doctrine: Religion and Theology in a Postliberal Age* (Philadelphia: Westminster, 1984), 36.

26. See Dykstra and Bass, "A Theological Understanding of Christian Practices," 17, and Sarah Coakley, "Deepening Practices: Perspectives from Ascetical and Mystical Theology," in Volf and Bass, eds., *Practicing Theology*, 78.

as an integral part of living a Christian life,[27] and, whether it occurs in academic or nonacademic settings, is an exercise in understanding. Which is where practices come in. Engagement in practices helps open our eyes to how core beliefs are to be understood and reformulated as Christians live in ever-changing situations.

What Grounds What?

Here is a stripped-down sketch of my argument so far: Christian beliefs normatively shape Christian practices, and engaging in practices can lead to acceptance and deeper understanding of these beliefs. The crucial issue that remains to be addressed is this: Do beliefs ground practices, or do practices ultimately ground beliefs? In one sense, this is not quite the right way to put the question. Are not beliefs — core Christian beliefs — an integral part of Christian practices? I have argued that they are. And yet we still have to inquire about the *status* of beliefs precisely as components of practices.

Contemporary academic and popular culture tends to subordinate beliefs to practices to the point of completely functionalizing beliefs. Pierre Hadot's important book *Philosophy as a Way of Life* might serve as an example. In his account, as in a qualified sense in my own, "the choice of a form of life" comes first. Philosophical discourse "gives justifications and theoretical foundations" for that choice.[28] Hadot rightly sees discourse not as an end in itself but in service of a way of life. Notice, however, how he understands the service proper to discourse. The choice of the form of life is "justified *after the fact* by a given systematic construction." Choosing the good is not a consequence of holding a set of true beliefs, but the other way around.[29]

27. See Kathryn Tanner, "Theological Reflection and Christian Practices," in Volf and Bass, eds., *Practicing Theology*, 228ff.

28. Pierre Hadot, *Philosophy as a Way of Life: Spiritual Exercises from Socrates to Foucault* (ed. Arnold I. Davidson; trans. Michael Chase; Oxford: Blackwell, 1995), 281.

29. Hadot, *Philosophy as a Way of Life*, 282-83. Commenting on Stoicism and Epicureanism, Hadot notes as mistaken the view that from the theories of Chrysipus or Epicurus "would spring, as if by accident one could say, a morality. But the reverse is

Would Hadot's account of the relation between "the choice of the good" and "philosophical discourse" work in theology as a model for the relation between Christian beliefs and Christian practices, between theology and a way of life? That depends on how one interprets Hadot. One could take him to mean that a set of beliefs will develop from a chronologically prior choice of the good. When such a set of beliefs does develop, it will be a *true* set of beliefs, capable of adequately grounding the choice of the good. The choice of the good would chronologically precede this set of beliefs, but this set of beliefs would logically ground the choice of the good.

Such a reading of Hadot's ordering of "beliefs" and "practices" would be analogous to the way in which, according to John Zizioulas, the doctrine of the Trinity emerged: ecclesial communal practice led the church to claim that communion of three divine persons is ontologically ultimate. But what made possible the emergence of the church and its claims about the ontological ultimacy of communion was, of course, the reality of the divine communion, which can be expressed in the form of true Trinitarian beliefs.[30] Whether or not one agrees with Zizioulas's account of the emergence of the doctrine of the Trinity, the more general understanding of the relation between beliefs and practices it instantiates is plausible.

It is unlikely, however, that giving chronological priority to a way of life and logical primacy to a set of beliefs would satisfy Hadot. He believes that the one and the same choice of the good can be "justified by extremely diverse philosophical discourses."[31] Depending on changing situations —

---

true. It is the abstract theories that are intended to justify the existential attitude. One could say, to express it otherwise, that every existential attitude implies a representation of the world that must necessarily be expressed in a discourse. But this discourse alone is not the philosophy, it is only an element of it, for the philosophy is first of all the existential attitude itself, accompanied by inner and outer discourses: the latter have as their role to express the representation of the world that is implied in such and such an existential attitude, and these discourses allow one at the same time to rationally justify the attitude and to communicate it to others" (quoted by Davidson in Hadot, *Philosophy as a Way of Life*, 30-31).

30. John Zizioulas, *Being as Communion: Studies in Personhood and the Church* (Crestwood, N.Y.: St. Vladimir's Seminary Press, 1985).

31. Hadot, *Philosophy as a Way of Life*, 212.

depending on reigning plausibilities — the set of beliefs will vary, and will do so in order to be able to "justify" a given choice of the good.

Will this do as a model for the relation between Christian beliefs and practices? There are theologians who think so.[32] Whether they are right depends a great deal on how one understands theology's relation to its primary subject matter, God. Practices, I have argued earlier, are Christian insofar as they are "resonances" of God's engagement with the world. But how should we understand "God's engagement with the world"? Above all, does such talk purport to sketch, in human conceptualities and therefore in a broken way, what is truly the case and what is in accord with God's self-revelation in Christ as attested in the Scriptures?

I take it that theology is not simply reflection about how communities of faith use language about God — not "critical talk about talk about God." God, not just human talk about God, is the proper object of theology. If this is so, then Christian beliefs about God are not analogous to Hadot's philosophical discourse. No doubt one's interest in God may be awakened and one's understanding of God will be deepened through engagement in practices. But we engage in practices for the sake of God; we don't construe a picture of God so as to justify engagement in a particular set of practices. As the highest good, God matters for God's own sake, not for the sake of a preferred way of life. Since we identify who God is through beliefs — primarily through the canonical witness to divine self-revelation — adequate beliefs about God cannot be ultimately grounded in a way of life; a way of life must be grounded in adequate beliefs about God.[33]

32. Consider, for instance, what Marianne Sawicki does with the creedal Christian claim that Jesus Christ is risen. She justifies it pragmatically: "The hungry little ones, always with the church, are the reason why the resurrection of Jesus must be affirmed as bodily, absolutely, for Christian faith" (Marianne Sawicki, *Seeing the Lord: Resurrection and Early Christian Practices* [Minneapolis: Fortress, 1994], 275).

33. The way Hadot relates the choice of a way of life and philosophical discourse is analogous to the way in which some liberation theologians relate praxis of social engagement and theological reflection. In his recent book on theological methodology, at the end of a long chapter on his own fruitful and decade-long engagement with various liberation theologies, Jürgen Moltmann asks the following critical question: "If praxis is the [ultimate] criterion of theory, what is the criterion of praxis?" (Jürgen Moltmann, *Experiences in Theology: Ways and Forms of Christian Theology* [trans. M. Kohl; Minneapolis: Fortress, 2000], 294).

If Christian beliefs ultimately ground Christian practices, theology cannot limit itself to explicating the significance of "God" and of what "God has done" for a way of life, but must concern itself with the disputed truth claims about God — and *do so precisely also for the sake of a way of life*. It matters, for instance, a great deal for a way of life whether human beings are God's creatures or God is a human creature, a projection of our greatest ideals or an imaginary rectifier of our own impotence. Ludwig Feuerbach, Karl Marx, and Friedrich Nietzsche rightly felt the need to offer alternative accounts of human history and of the cosmos to the one they inherited from the Christian tradition in the light of their persuasion that God is a human creation, and not the other way around.

To be concerned with truth claims about God means also to be interested in how beliefs about God and God's relation to the world *fit* among themselves and with other beliefs human beings hold. The fit between Christian beliefs may be very tight (say, such that one can reduce all of them to a single complex belief) or rather loose (say, such that one can situate them in a narrative framework or a set of factually related but logically independent narrative frameworks),[34] but fit they must. If the truth of the Christian faith matters, then the way you understand the Lord's Supper must fit with your account of Christ's death, and this must fit with your doctrine of the Trinity, and all of it must fit with the way you understand the nature and predicament of human beings.

Moreover, since Christian beliefs coexist with a host of other beliefs about the world — from claims about the future of the universe to theories about the kind of work neurons do in human brains — the question of the relationship of Christian beliefs to all these other beliefs must also be posed. Theology must pursue the question of truth and must do so in conjunction with, and not in isolation from, other disciplines. In a word, because Christian beliefs relate to everyday practices as a fitted set of beliefs with a claim to express truth about God and God's relation to the world, theologians must be concerned with more than just how beliefs

---

34. In *Eccentric Existence: A Theological Anthropology* (Louisville: Westminster John Knox, 2009), David Kelsey argues powerfully for reading the Scriptures as containing three factually intertwined but logically independent narratives.

relate to everyday practices — and must be so concerned precisely *for the sake of* everyday practices.

The Apostle Paul, Theology, Practices

The apostle Paul was arguably the first Christian theologian and certainly the most influential of the early Christian theologians. In conclusion it may be instructive to compare briefly the model I have developed above of theology's relation to a way of life with Paul's way of theologizing. True, contemporary theologians are in some important ways unlike Paul: the risen Lord has appeared to Paul, and his writings have a canonical status to us. This makes beliefs even more critical in our theologizing than they were in Paul's. That said, Paul's and our theological tasks are arguably analogous.

There is a long history of New Testament scholars' making what I think is on the whole a mistaken distinction in Paul's writings between the "indicative" and the "imperative" sections. In this distinction, the indicative sections come first; they are doctrinal (they explicate Christian beliefs) and foundational. The imperative sections come second; they are ethical (they admonish to Christian practices) and are of secondary importance because they are grounded in beliefs. Beliefs can and should be explicated in their own right, without relation to practices; practices can be understood only in relation to beliefs. According to this picture, Paul operated with something analogous to the accepted disciplinary distinctions between "systematic theology" on the one side and ethics and "practical theology" on the other, as well as with the corresponding clear demarcation between "self-standing" beliefs and "derived" practices.

Not everything is wrong with this picture. As the momentous "therefore" in Romans 12:1 attests ("I appeal to you therefore, brothers and sisters, by the mercies of God, to present your bodies as a living sacrifice"), beliefs about God and what God has done do serve for Paul to justify ways in which Christians relate among themselves and with outsiders. And yet, to let the matter rest at that is to simplify things to the point of distortion. As Troels Engberg-Pedersen has shown in *Paul and the Stoics,* the parenetic sections in Paul do not simply follow the doctrinal sections; rather, "at the most fundamental level and from one end to the other" his letters are an "exercise in parenesis." "Parenesis has two components," a doctrinal and ethical one, for it consists "in Paul's *reminding* his addressees of what *has* happened and his *appeal* to them to put it into *practice*."[35]

Significantly, the description of what has happened — what God has done and what God will do for Paul and his readers — is "tilted towards what we may call its anthropological side: towards what the 'objective' Christ event set going by God has meant to Paul and his addressees." The "tilting" is present because Paul offers what God has done "as a basis for his appeal to them [his addressees] to put it into practice." So in Paul beliefs *as beliefs* are practice-shaping. Yet he does not consider beliefs to be justifications *after the fact* of a way of life. As Engberg-Pedersen puts it, "The 'objective' framework remains very solidly in place, of course. It is *God* who *has* done something in the Christ event and God and Christ who *will* do something in the future."[36]

Paul had a realistic perspective on what God has done for humanity, as Engberg-Pedersen recognizes. At the same time, he suggests that we, Paul's contemporary interpreters, reduce Paul's claims about God and God's relation to the world to "metaphysical 'constructions' whose function is to give ontological substance" to his ethical ideas.[37] Engberg-Pedersen's suggestion on how to appropriate the teaching of Paul is structurally similar to Hadot's recommendation on how to appropriate ancient spiritual exercises: he discards ancient justifying philosophical discourses and keeps the moral vision.

For Christian theology, this will not do. Such an account of the status of beliefs would be deeply at odds with the nature of Christian practices themselves. For these are done precisely in response to what God has done for the life of the world, which is what Christian core beliefs seek to express. Like Paul, we should resolutely place theology in the service of practices and precisely for this reason concentrate our reflection on

35. Troels Engberg-Pedersen, *Paul and the Stoics* (Louisville: Westminster John Knox, 2000), 294.

36. Engberg-Pedersen, *Paul and the Stoics*, 295.

37. Engberg-Pedersen, *Paul and the Stoics*, 30.

God, for whose sake we live a Christian way of life and therefore, as theologians, engage in explicating Christian beliefs.

Will theology so conceived have sufficiently to do with "real" life? Not nearly as much as the God for whose sake we are theologians, but more than enough, I believe, to satisfy the concerns of those who are justly troubled by theology's seeming irrelevance.

PART II

Communities of Faith in a Pluralistic World

CHAPTER THREE

Soft Difference:
Church and Culture in 1 Peter

⎯⎯⎯⎯ ∞∞∞ ⎯⎯⎯⎯

Gospel, Culture, Church

As much as anyone else during the past one hundred years, the German theologian Ernst Troeltsch has shaped contemporary thinking on gospel and culture. To give just one example, probably the most influential book on the topic in the English-speaking world, H. Richard Niebuhr's classic historical and theological study *Christ and Culture,* "in one sense undertakes no more than to supplement and in part to correct" Troeltsch's work on *The Social Teaching of the Christian Churches.*[1] Why did Troeltsch earn such a wide hearing?

Following in the footsteps of sociologist Max Weber, Troeltsch developed a very influential distinction between "church" and "sect" (and added his own third category of "mystic," which I will leave aside here because my interest is in Christian community). As Weber suggested, the distinction runs something like this: you *get born* into the church; you *join* a sect; like a good mother, the church will embrace you irrespective of your behavior; like a stern father, the sect will make you follow a strict ethical code.[2]

---

1. H. Richard Niebuhr, *Christ and Culture* (New York: Harper & Brothers, 1951), x.
2. See Max Weber, "Die protestantischen Sekten und der Geist des Kapitalismus,"

Weber's distinction between church and sect was supposed to be a strictly sociological distinction that provided models of how religious groups relate to the larger world. Going beyond Weber, Troeltsch made the simple but astute observation that one cannot separate theology from sociology. The church, which wishes to embrace all of its sons and daughters, will invariably proclaim "grace"; the sect, to which only an elite number belong, will stress "law." The church will affirm the "world"; the sect will deny the "world" by retreating from it or occasionally attacking it. The church will seek power in the world, and to achieve it, make the necessary compromises; the sect will insist on undiluted purity and remain on the margins. The church will stress sacraments and education; the sect will value conversion and commitment.

By analyzing the teachings of church and sect through the centuries, in his magisterial *The Social Teaching of the Christian Churches* Troeltsch concluded that "the whole Christian world of thought and dogma" depends "on the fundamental sociological conditions, on the idea of fellowship which was dominant at any given time."[3] Troeltsch was no social determinist; after all, he believed that the "idea" of Christianity gave rise to all three social forms — church, sect, and mystic — in which the Christian faith was lived out through the centuries. Yet these social forms in turn shaped Christian doctrine, the very center of it. For instance, the Christ of a church is different from the Christ of a sect: the first is a gracious "redeemer," the second is a commanding "Lord." Similar kinds of differences between church and sect can be observed with respect to other doctrines too. One might disagree with Troeltsch on particular points, but his thesis as a whole makes sense. The beliefs and practices of a Christian community are inextricably bound to its character as a social reality; when you change one, sooner or later you will change the other too.

Notice the implications of Troeltsch's thesis about the interrelation of Christian communities' social forms and their doctrines and practices

---

in *Gesammelte Aufsätze zur Religionssoziologie* I (Tübingen: J. C. B. Mohr [Paul Siebeck], 1963), 207-36.

3. Ernst Troeltsch, *The Social Teaching of the Christian Churches* (trans. Olive Wyon; London: George Allen & Unwin, 1931), 2:994.

for the topic of gospel and culture. "Gospel" is never simply "the good news," not even the good news supported by a web of beliefs. "Gospel" always involves a way of living in a given social environment as a Christian community (in a broad sense, including various degrees of commitment). To ask about how the gospel relates to culture is to ask how to live as a Christian *community* in a particular cultural context. Reflection on gospel and culture will be truncated without reflection on church and culture. Indeed, there is no other way to reflect adequately on gospel and culture except by reflecting on how the social embodiments of the gospel relate to a given culture.

Church and culture is the topic I wish to address. I want to explore the nature of Christian communal presence in contemporary societies and the character of Christian identity and difference. To that end I will engage in what might be called "theological and sociological exegesis" of one key biblical book on the topic — 1 Peter. Methodologically, I will neither examine simply the text of 1 Peter nor simply the situation of the addressees, the Petrine community. Rather, I am interested in the reactions of the author to the situation. I am assuming, however, that, though absent from the community, in a profound sense the author of 1 Peter is still a part of it.

But why 1 Peter? In *Christ and Culture* Niebuhr seeks to indicate how the various types of relation between Christ and culture that he finds in the history of the church are exemplified in various texts produced by the early Christian communities. "Christ against culture" is best expressed in 1 John, "the Christ of culture" in Gnostic writings, "Christ above culture" in some motifs in Matthew's Gospel (such as rendering to Caesar the things that are Caesar's), "Christ and culture in paradox" in the Pauline writings, and "Christ the transformer of culture" in the Fourth Gospel.

I should say that I find Niebuhr's typology enticing but unpersuasive, and his treatment of the New Testament texts is skewed. But this point is not the one I wish to dwell on here. What interests me more is the observation that the one text which speaks more pointedly and comprehensively to the problem of "Christ and culture" than any other in the New Testament is conspicuously absent from Niebuhr's account. I am referring to 1 Peter, the epistle whose main theme is Christian life in a non-

Christian environment.[4] I am not sure about the reasons for this omission on Niebuhr's part. But I am quite sure that 1 Peter bursts not only Niebuhr's five neat models of how Christ relates to culture, but also Troeltsch's distinction between church and sect.

Aliens and Sojourners

As Reinhard Feldmeier has argued recently, the key metaphor that 1 Peter employs to express the Christian relationship to culture is the metaphor of "aliens" (*paroikos* and *parepidēmos*).[5] It takes only a brief glance through the history of the church to see its potency. By the second century being "alien" had become central to the self-understanding of Christians. Later it was essential to monastic and Anabaptist movements alike, to Augustine and Zinzendorf, and, in our own time, to Dietrich Bonhoeffer *(The Cost of Discipleship)* no less than to Jim Wallis *(Sojourners)* or Stanley Hauerwas *(Resident Aliens)*.

The metaphor "aliens" had such a powerful influence because it sums up central themes from the Hebrew Scriptures and expresses some fundamental perspectives from the whole New Testament about the problem of Christian identity and difference. Abraham was called to go from his country, his kindred, and his father's house (Gen. 12:1). His grandchildren and the children of his grandchildren became "aliens in the land of Egypt" (Lev. 19:34), and the nation of which he and Sarah were parents lived as exiles in the Babylonian captivity. And even when they were secure in their own land, Yahweh their God demanded of them to be different from the surrounding nations.

The root of Christian self-understanding as aliens and sojourners lies not so much in the story of Abraham and Sarah and the nation of Israel as it does in the destiny of Jesus Christ, his mission and his rejection, which ultimately brought him to the cross. "He came to what was his

4. See Leonard Goppelt, *Der erste Petrusbrief* (KEK XII/1; Göttingen: Vandenhoeck & Ruprecht, 1978), 41.

5. Reinhard Feldmeier, *Die Christen als Fremde: Die Metapher der Fremde in der Antiken Welt, im Urchristentum und im 1. Petrusbrief* (Tübingen: J. C. B. Mohr [Paul Siebeck], 1992).

own, and his own people did not accept him" (John 1:11). He was a stranger to the world because the world into which he came was estranged from God. And so it is with his followers. "When a person becomes a believer, then he (or she) moves from the far country to the vicinity of God. . . . There now arises a relation of reciprocal foreignness and estrangement between Christians and the world."[6] Christians are born of the Spirit (John 3:8) and are therefore not "from the world" but, like Jesus Christ, "from God" (John 15:19).

There is no need here to give a detailed analysis of the trajectory from Abraham and the people of Israel to Jesus Christ and his church. It will suffice to take a careful look at the metaphor "aliens" in 1 Peter. Yet to understand the metaphor, an analysis of the terms *paroikos* and *parepidēmos,* say of an etymological or even sociological kind, will not do. In 1 Peter these terms mean no more and no less than *what the epistle as a whole teaches about the relation of Christians to the surrounding culture.* To unpack "aliens" we need to broaden our vision and look at what the epistle as a whole says about the nature of Christian presence in a given culture.

On the matter of Christians living in a non-Christian environment, 1 Peter is not simply one little voice among other New Testament voices. Though the epistle is marginal within the New Testament as a whole, it pulls together "essential social-ethical traditions" of the whole New Testament.[7] A careful reader will, however, discover in 1 Peter not only a "compiler," but also a creative thinker in his own right, capable of integrating the social features Troeltsch tells us we should find clearly separated and assigned to different social types of religious communities.

Eschatological Difference

The designation of Christians as *paroikoi* and *parepidēmoi* (1 Pet. 1:1; 2:11) implies, without a doubt, a "clear distance in relation to society, a dis-

6. Gustaf Stählin, "Xenos," in *Theological Dictionary of the New Testament* (trans. and ed. Geoffrey W. Bromiley; Grand Rapids: Eerdmans, 1964-76), 5:29.
7. Leonard Goppelt, "Prinzipien neutestamentlicher und systematischer Sozialethik heute," in *Die Verantwortung der Kirche in der Gesellschaft* (ed. Jörg Baur et al.; Stuttgart: Calwer Verlag, 1972), 16.

tance from its values and ideals, from its institutions and politics."[8] What does the distance mean, however? Distance in what sense, and for what reason?

In his well-known sociological and exegetical study, John H. Elliott advocated a thesis that the term *paroikoi* describes the social marginalization that Christians experienced before conversion. In the church they then found a protective *oikos* and were provided with an ideological self-understanding as the new eschatological people of God.[9] The "homeless" found the warmth of an ecclesial home. That may well have been the case — provided one does not understand ideology in a purely functional manner, without reference to the truth content of the claims it contains.[10]

This helpful sociological perspective is, however, one-sided in a crucial respect. While it rightly perceives the estrangement that a Christian way of life — or Christian "ideology" — might help to overcome, it underestimates the *new estrangement that a Christian way of life creates.*[11] That the members of the Petrine community might have become Christians because many of them were socially marginalized seems an intelligent hypothesis. That they became alienated from their social environment in a new way when they became Christians is what the episode explicitly states.[12] Before conversion, they were much like their neighbors (see 4:3ff.); after conversion they became different, and this difference was the cause of their persecution.[13] Since our topic here is not the psycho-

---

8. Feldmeier, *Die Christen als Fremde*, 22.

9. John H. Elliott, *A Home for the Homeless: A Sociological Exegesis of 1 Peter, Its Situation and Strategy* (Philadelphia: Fortress, 1981), 21-58, 129-32. Cf. John H. Elliott, "1 Peter, Its Situation and Strategy: A Discussion with David Balch," in *Perspectives on 1 Peter* (ed. C. H. Talbert; Macon, Ga.: Mercer, 1986), 67-68.

10. So Elliott, *A Home for the Homeless*, 268.

11. This is a systematic one-sidedness, endemic to functionalist sociological explanations; they are unable to perceive religious beliefs and practices as independent social forces. For a critique of sociological functionalism in exegesis see John Milbank, *Theology and Social Theory: Beyond Secular Reason* (Oxford: Blackwell, 1990), 111-21.

12. Elliott recognizes this phenomenon but underplays its importance. See Elliott, "1 Peter, Its Situation and Strategy."

13. In persecution the issues of both difference and justice are involved. In 1 Peter persecution is first of all a problem of difference — people became Christians and as a

sociology of conversion but the nature of *Christian* presence in the world, I will concentrate on this new distance that arises from becoming a Christian.

It would be a mistake, however, to describe this new distance as simply *religious.* In that case, the terms "aliens" and "sojourners" would have been used purely metaphorically and would indicate "no actual social condition of the addressees."[14] Such a view would presume that religion is essentially a strictly private affair, touching only the deep region of a person's heart. Surely this is a mistaken view. That religion takes place simply between a naked soul and its divinity is a prejudice, one which is nourished today by the fact that in modern societies until recently religion has been pushed outside the public arena. Yet even in the so-called private sphere — such as personal life, family, or friendships — religion *continues to be a social force.*[15] Religion is essentially a way of thinking and of living within a larger social context. Religious distance from the world is therefore always social distance. At least this holds true for Christian faith.

How does this Christian distance from society that is religious and social come about? First Peter answers: through *the new birth into the living hope.* "Blessed be the God and Father of our Lord Jesus Christ! By his great mercy he has given us a new birth into the living hope through the resurrection of Jesus Christ from the dead" (1:3). The new birth, whose subject is the merciful and electing God (1:2), creates a twofold distance. First, it is a *new* birth. It distances one from the old way of life, inherited from one's ancestors (1:18) and transmitted by the culture at large — a way of life characterized by the lack of knowledge of God and by misguided desires (1:14). Second, it is a birth into a *living hope.* It distances

---

consequence encountered "blaspheming" and were subjected to "fiery ordeal" (4:4, 12). Injustice here seems secondary to the difference, a result of the intolerance toward "the other" and of the attempt to suppress its difference.

14. A view rightly criticized by Elliott (*Home for the Homeless,* 131). Elliott seems to assume, however, that if the terms "aliens" and "sojourners" are not meant metaphorically, they must describe the social situation of Christians before conversion. But there is no reason the terms could not describe Christians' social situation *after* conversion.

15. For a brief analysis of the discussion on privatization of religion see Hubert Knoblauch, "Die Verflüchtigung der Religion ins Religiöse: Thomas Luckmans Unsichtbare Religion," in *Die Unsichtbare Religion* (ed. Thomas Luckman; Frankfurt a.M.: Suhrkamp, 1991), 19ff.

one from the transitoriness of the present world, in which all human efforts ultimately end in death. In more abstract theological terms, the new birth into the living hope frees people from the meaninglessness of sin and hopelessness of death.

This process of distancing by rebirth takes place through redemption by the blood of the Lamb (1:19) and through the resurrection of Jesus Christ from the dead (1:3). People who are born into the living hope take part in the eschatological process that started with the coming of Jesus Christ into this world, with his ministry of word and deed, and with his death and his resurrection. Christian difference from the social environment is therefore an *eschatological* one. In the midst of the world in which Christians live, they are given a new home that comes from God's future. The new birth commences a journey to this home.

Notice the significance of the new birth for Christian social identity. Christians do not come into their social world from outside seeking either to accommodate to their new home (like second-generation immigrants would), shape it in the image of the one they have left behind (like colonizers would), or establish a little haven in the strange new world reminiscent of the old (as resident aliens would). They are not outsiders who either seek to become insiders or maintain strenuously the status of outsiders. Christians are the *insiders* who have diverted from their culture by being born again. They are by definition those who are not what they used to be, those who do not live like they used to live. In social terms, Christian difference is therefore not an insertion of something new into the old from outside, but a bursting out of the new *precisely within the proper space of the old.*

The question of how to live in a non-Christian environment, then, does not translate simply into the question of whether one adopts or rejects the social practices of the environment. This question is asked by outsiders, who have the luxury of observing a culture from a vantage point that is external to that culture. Christians do not have such a vantage point since they have experienced a new birth as inhabitants of a particular culture. Hence they are in an important sense insiders. As those who are a part of the environment from which they have diverted by having been born again and whose difference is therefore socially internal to that environment, Christians ask, "Which beliefs and practices of the culture that is ours must we reject now that our self has been re-constituted by new birth? Which can we retain? What must we reshape to reflect better the values of God's new creation?"

Ecclesial Difference

Talk about "new birth" could suggest a purely individual process of distancing from the culture — a soul takes flight from the world, seeks refuge with the eternal God, and becomes a stranger to the world of sin and death in that it migrates *(metoikizō)* into its undefiled and imperishable inheritance (1:4).[16] If this were what was meant by "new birth," Christian difference would be strictly private; Gnosticism and mysticism would thrive under the name-brand "Christianity." Does the text of 1 Peter support such an understanding of new birth, however?

The new birth "of the imperishable seed, through the living and enduring word of God" (1:23), is not simply an internal and private event. Think of its inextricable connection with baptism. Some exegetes surmise that the whole epistle is a baptismal liturgy.[17] Be that as it may, a connection between new birth and baptism is undeniable — a fact with momentous consequences. No one can baptize himself or herself; everyone must be baptized by another person into a given Christian community. Baptism is an *incorporation* into the body of Christ, a doorway into a Christian community. Baptism will not do the distancing for you, but it will tell you that genuine Christian distance has ecclesial shape. It is lived in a community that lives as "aliens" in a larger social environment.

The new birth is neither a conversion to our authentic inner self nor a migration *(metoikesia)* of the soul into a heavenly realm, but a translation of a person into the house of God *(oikos tou theou)* erected in the midst of the world. It comes as no surprise, then, to find in 1 Peter that the Hebrew Scriptures' *collective* designations for the people of God are applied to the Christian church: "But you are a chosen race, a royal

16. For "migration" as a philosophical category see Peter Sloterdijk, *Weltfremdheit* (Frankfurt a.M.: Suhrkamp, 1993), 80ff.

17. For a discussion see J. N. D. Kelly, *A Commentary on the Epistles of Peter and Jude* (New York: Harper & Row, 1969), 15ff.

priesthood, a holy nation, God's one people" (2:9). The distance from the social environment in 1 Peter is not simply eschatological; it is also *essentially ecclesiological.*[18] Its correlate is the eschatological *people of God,* who live in the world hoping for God's new creation, not "our own authentic little voice" or some "heavenly home" separated from this world by an unbridgeable gulf.

Correspondingly, one must understand the "walk" *(anastrophē)* of Christians so strongly emphasized in 1 Peter (1:15, 17-18; 2:12; 3:1-2, 16) not as private morality instructing how to purify the soul from an evil world or how to "love yourself and be gentle with yourself . . . take care of each other,"[19] but as an *ecclesial way of being* that is distinct from the way of being of the society at large. "Walk" is the way the *Christian community* lives in the world. Wherever Christians find themselves — alone or with other believers — a Christian *social* difference is manifested there. Communities of those who are born anew and follow Christ live an alternative way of life within the political, ethnic, religious, and cultural institutions of the larger society.

We get no sense from 1 Peter, however, that the church should strive to regulate all domains of social life and reshape society in the image of the heavenly Jerusalem. One could argue, of course, that it would be anachronistic to expect such a thought even to occur in the Petrine community. Were they not discriminated against, a minority living in premodern times? But notwithstanding the experience of discrimination, the Petrine community betrays no trace of an aggressive sect in the sense meant by Ernst Troeltsch. It did not wish to impose itself or the kingdom of God on the world, but to live in faithfulness to God and to the values of God's kingdom, while inviting others to do the same. It had no desire to do to others what they did not want done to them. It had no covert totalitarian agenda. Rather, the community was to live an alternative way of life in the present social setting, transforming it, as it could, from within. In any case, the community did not seek to exert social or political pressure, but to give pubic witness to a new way of life.

18. So also Feldmeier, *Die Christen als Fremde,* 188.

19. Robert N. Bellah et al., *Habits of the Heart: Individualism and Commitment in American Life* (Berkeley: University of California Press, 1996), 221.

Difference and Identity

Celsus, the most significant critic of Christianity in the second century, wrote: "If all men wanted to be Christians, the Christians would no longer want them."[20] In fact he insisted that Christians were so fascinated with rejecting what is common to all people that they themselves would no longer want to be Christians if everyone decided to become one. In his view, the primary point of reference for Christian identity was the non-Christian world. Christian identity is established through the negative activity of setting oneself apart from others. Christian distance from society is a spiteful difference for the sake of difference, nourished by a deep-seated resentment against the dominant social order, which rejected them. Is this picture what we find in 1 Peter?

There is no doubt that 1 Peter stresses the church's difference from its social environment. This difference is what the metaphor "aliens" suggests and what surfaces repeatedly throughout the epistle.[21] But what is the significance of this observation for the nature of Christian identity? I suggest that the crucial question is not to what degree one stresses difference, but rather on what basis Christian identity is established. Identity can be forged through two related but clearly distinct processes: either through a negative process of rejecting the beliefs and practices of others, or through a positive process of giving allegiance to something distinctive. It is significant that 1 Peter consistently establishes the difference positively, not negatively. There are no direct injunctions not to behave as non-Christians do. Rather, the exhortation to be different centers primarily on the positive example of a holy God (1:15f.) and of the suffering Christ (2:21ff.). This approach is surprising, especially given the situation of social conflict in which the Petrine community was engaged. We expect injunctions to reject the ways of the world; instead we find admonitions to follow the path of Christ.

Let me reinforce this point by looking at two images of evil in 1 Peter: the *devil* and *fleshly desires*. The author of 1 Peter does not warn in totalizing discourse against an evil world, but calls the community to re-

20. Celsus in Origen, *Contra Celsum* 3.9.
21. See Elliott, *A Home for the Homeless,* 120.

sist the devil, who prowls around, looking for someone to devour (5:8). The image of a prowling devil suggests that evil is not some impenetrable all-encompassing darkness outside the walls of the church, equally thick in all places; rather, evil is a mobile force, something one always has to deal with but is never quite sure where and how it will be encountered. The statements that celebrate Christian calling "out of darkness into his marvelous light" notwithstanding (2:9), 1 Peter does not operate with the stark opposition between "divine community" and "satanic world." Correspondingly, the author seems less interested in hurling threats against unbelieving and aggressive non-Christian neighbors[22] than in celebrating Christians' special status before God (see 2:9f.). Christian hope, not the damnation of non-Christians, figures centrally in the letter (see 1:3; 3:15).[23]

When we encounter negative examples of how Christians should not behave, then our attention is drawn not so much to the lifestyle of non-Christians as to "the *desires of the flesh* that wage war against the soul" (2:11). These are, as 1 Peter points out explicitly, the former desires of Christians themselves.[24] The force of the injunction is not "Do not be as your neighbors are!" but "Do not be as *you were!*"[25] This perspective fits

---

22. Talk about judgment in 4:17 is not a proof to the contrary. Peter writes: "For the time has come for the judgment to begin with the household of God; if it begins with us, what will be the end of those who do not obey the gospel of God?" Notice, however, that the church as the house of God is not spared judgment. Judgment is here an inclusive, not an exclusive, category. It is interesting to observe in this context that 1 Peter comes closest of all the New Testament writings to entertaining the possibility that deceased non-Christians might be able to make a decision for Christ after death (4:6; Goppelt, *Der erste Petrusbrief,* 277f.).

23. See Norbert Brox, *Der erste Petrusbrief* (EKKNT 21; Zürich/Neukirchen-Vluyn: Benzinger/Neukirchener, 1979), 16. The cryptic passage in which we are told that non-Christians were "destined" to disobey the word points, however, in a different direction (2:8).

24. See Goppelt, *Der erste Petrusbrief,* 117.

25. One can read 1 Peter 4:2 as an exhortation not to live like non-Christians: ". . . so as to live for the rest of your earthly life no longer by human desires but by the will of God." The text speaks, however, about "*human* desires" inclusively, not of the desires of the "world" or of non-Christians, though these desires are "the desires of the flesh" (2:11) and therefore the desires that Christians "formerly had" (1:14). Moreover, not living by human desires depends on the *positive* injunction to arm "yourself also with the same intention" as Christ (4:1). First Peter transcends the simple schema of "pure church"

with the observation that the new birth distances people first of all from their old, culturally shaped self and in this way from the world. This logic is what the metaphor of new birth suggests and is also what 1 Peter explicitly states: "you were ransomed from *your* futile ways inherited from your ancestors" (1:18). What permeates the epistle is not a fixation on distance from the world, but enthusiasm about the eschatological future.

It is Christian identity that creates difference from the social environment, not the other way around. The faith of the Petrine community is nourished more on its own intrinsic vision than on deprecatory stories about others.[26] Let me reinforce this point by an observation. When identity is forged primarily through the negative process of the rejection of the beliefs and practices of others, violence seems unavoidable, especially in situations of conflict. We have to push others away from ourselves and keep them at a distance, and we have to close ourselves off from others to keep ourselves pure of their taint. The violence of pushing and keeping away can express itself in subdued resentment, or it can break out in aggressive and destructive behavior. The Petrine community was discriminated against and even comprised a persecuted minority. Feelings of rage and thoughts of revenge must have been lurking as a threat, ready to rise up either in aggression toward their enemies or at least in relishing the thought of their future damnation. But what do we find in 1 Peter? Exhortation is given not to repay evil for evil or abuse for abuse, but to *repay evil with a blessing* (3:9)! From the perspective of pop psychology or quasi-revolutionary rhetoric, such a refusal to vent the rage and actuate the mechanism of revenge would be at best described as unhealthy and at worst thought of as worthy only of "despicable rubble."[27] In fact, it speaks of sovereign serenity and sets a profound revolution in motion. When blessing replaces rage and revenge, the one who suffers violence refuses to retaliate in kind and chooses instead to en-

---

versus "sinful world"; the desires do not simply reign among non-Christians, but also wage war against the souls of Christians (see 2:11).

26. On this distinction see the brief (and somewhat too stark) comments of Charles Taylor, "Comparison, History, Truth," in *Myth and Philosophy* (ed. F. Reynolds and David Tracy; New York: SUNY, 1990), 54.

27. See Karl Marx, *Karl Marx/Friedrich Engels Werke*, vol. 4 (Berlin: Dietz Verlag, 1978), 200.

counter violence with an embrace. But how can people give up violence in the midst of a life-threatening conflict if their identity is wrapped up in rejecting the beliefs and practices of their enemies? Only those who refuse to be defined by their enemies can bless them.

Difference and Acculturation

There is a strange tension in 1 Peter between the stress on difference and attempts at acculturation. This tension has given rise to opposing interpretations of the purpose of the letter as a whole. The dominant metaphor, "aliens," clearly underlines the difference. John H. Elliott latches onto the metaphor and argues that the main purpose of 1 Peter is to protect Christian identity in an unfriendly environment. "The Petrine strategy was," he writes, "to avert . . . forces of social disintegration through a reinforcement of the distinctive identity of the Christian community."[28] On the other hand, if one looks at the so-called "household codes" and compares them with similar material from the Hellenistic tradition, then it seems that interest in difference gives way to attempts at acculturation. David L. Balch argues that the household codes unmistakably manifest 1 Peter's interest in accommodation. He concludes: "The author of 1 Peter wrote to advise Christians who were being persecuted about how they might become socially-politically acceptable to their society."[29]

Elliott's and Balch's thought moves within the framework of the alternative: either difference or acculturation (though both authors are aware that both processes were going on at the same time). Behind such a stance seems to be the persuasion that the community of 1 Peter was a "sect" which, in order to survive, either had to assert itself under pressure to assimilate or accommodate under the threat of persecution. Yet why focus on alternatives? If both difference and accommodation were tak-

28. Elliott, *A Home for the Homeless,* 217.
29. David L. Balch, *Let Wives Be Submissive: The Domestic Code in I Peter* (Society of Biblical Literature Monograph Series 26; Chico, Calif.: Scholars Press, 1981), 88. Balch later qualifies his position to mean that acculturation is the purpose of the household codes only, not of the letter as a whole (see David L. Balch, "Hellenization/Acculturation in 1 Peter," in *Perspectives on 1 Peter* [ed. C. H. Talbert; Macon, Ga.: Mercer, 1986], 82).

ing place at the same time, would it not be more fruitful to ask how the processes were combined? The focus on the combination of difference and acculturation would assume on the part of the Petrine community, however, a nonsectarian distance from their social environment: one is free from the pressure either simply to reject or affirm the surrounding culture.[30] Indeed, if I am correct that the distance from the social environment is in 1 Peter primarily a positive one resulting less from the rejection of the world than from the experience of the new birth to a living hope, then we can expect the epistle to transcend these unhelpful alternatives. We would have to take into account the possibility of either rejecting or accommodating to particular aspects of the surrounding culture in a piecemeal fashion. This approach is, I believe, what we actually find in 1 Peter.

In order to support this claim, I want to look at the so-called "household codes," the material that according to David L. Balch clearly demonstrates a Petrine strategy of accommodation. I want to argue that the "household codes" in 1 Peter are in fact an example of differentiated acceptance and rejection of the surrounding culture.

If one considers only the repeated injunctions to "subordinate oneself" (2:13, 18; 3:1), to suffer injustice (2:19), or to be gentle and tender (3:4, 8), then it could seem that in 1 Peter "Greek politics" is indeed celebrating victory over "the Mosaic story of salvation," the prophetic tradition, and the teachings of Jesus, as Balch claims.[31] One should not forget, however, the social and theological context of these statements. First, in 1 Peter the conservative "Hellenistic" instructions do not pertain to the relationships within the church (as do the household codes proper in Ephesians and Colossians), but to the relationship of Christians to non-Christians.[32] Second, Christians were involved in a conflict that they did not provoke, that they could not avoid, and in which they were the oppressed party. Third, an inalienable dimension of their communal iden-

---

30. In the case of simple rejection one would fall into what psychologists call "negative dependence," and in the case of simple affirmation one would not yet be free from "positive dependence." In both cases behavioral patterns would be determined from the outside.

31. Balch, "Hellenization/Acculturation in 1 Peter," 97-98.

32. So Feldmeier, *Die Christen als Fremde,* 161.

tity was a commitment to love of enemies and to nonviolence. Taken together, these three considerations place the "conservative" exhortation in a new light. To be "subject" means to act in the freedom of the slaves of God (2:16) and, instead of provoking additional acts of violence, to curb violence by doing good (knowing all along that suffering will be one's lot, because one cannot count on the victory of good over evil in the world). To be "subject" in a situation of conflict means to follow in the footsteps of the crucified Messiah, to refuse to take part in the automatism of revenge[33] — "evil for evil or abuse for abuse" (3:9) — and to break the vicious cycle of violence by suffering violence. If the injunction to be subject appears at first to function as a religious legitimization of oppression, it turns out, in fact, to be *a call to struggle against the politics of violence in the name of the politics of the crucified Messiah.* How blinded must one be by the prejudices of one's own liberal culture to see in this demanding way of suffering only accommodation to the dominant norms of the Hellenistic world!

Yet even when we are ready to accept that "subjection" — in politics, economics, and the home — can be an expression of radical Christianity rather than denial of Christian faith, we are still deeply troubled about how natural it seems for 1 Peter to accept the oppressive rule of the powerful — of the emperor and his governors (2:13ff.), of the slave master (2:18ff.), and of the husband (3:1ff.). True, 1 Peter provides them with no theological legitimization; we read nowhere in the epistle that the powerful were placed in their positions by God and that they are doing God's work (see Rom 13:1-7). Moreover, 1 Peter is sensitive to the possible injustice of the existing order.[34] Contrary to Aristotle, who believed that "there can be no injustice" toward slaves,[35] 1 Peter explicitly states that Christian slaves were suffering unjustly (2:19).

Still, we sense no desire to call into question the oppressive social order. Why? Is this lack on account of the minority status of the first Christians? (How could we change anything?!) Is it on account of the expectation of Jesus' imminent coming (4:7)? (Why should we bother, when

33. See Hannah Arendt, *The Human Condition* (Chicago: The University of Chicago Press, 1958), 240-41.

34. Feldmeier, *Die Christen als Fremde,* 162, 166.

35. Aristotle, *Nicomachean Ethics,* 11134b 9ff.

God's new creation is around the corner?!) Is it on account of a premodern understanding of social realities? (This order is how things always were and how they always will be!) Possibly all three factors are relevant. In any case, it seems clear that 1 Peter accommodates to the existing social realities as well as calling them into question. We should keep in mind, however, that the call to follow the crucified Messiah was, in the long run, much more effective in changing the unjust political, economic, and familial structures than direct exhortations to revolutionize them would ever have been. For an allegiance to the crucified Messiah — indeed, worship of a crucified God — is an eminently political act that subverts a politics of dominion at its very core.[36]

Today, we might reason, in contemporary democratic societies we must engage the structures of oppression directly. Social structures are made by human beings and, if unjust, must be unmade by them. That we are ready to act is admirable; that we have an urge to reshape and reconfigure everything might be dangerous. Stephen Toulmin has noted in *Cosmopolis* a feature of modernity that he called "The Myth of the Clean Slate."[37] Just as one can be rational only if one "demolishes all that was there before and starts from scratch," so one can be revolutionary only if one refashions the political situation from the ground up.[38] For example, the French Revolution "reached into everything. . . . it re-created time and space. . . . [T]he revolutionaries divided time into units that they took to be rational and natural. There were ten days to a week, three weeks to a month, and twelve months to a year."[39] For modernity social change is the enactment of a master narrative that the prophets of the new age have written on a clean sheet of paper.

36. Carl Schmitt, *Politische Theologie II. Die Legende von der Erledigung jeder Politischen Theologie* (Berlin: Duncker & Humbolt, 1970), 118, n. 3. Cf. Jürgen Moltmann, "Theologische Kritik der Politischen Religion," in *Kirche im Prozess der Aufklärung: Aspekte einer neuen "politischen Theologie"* (ed. J. B. Metz, J. Moltmann, and W. Oelmüller; München: Kaiser, 1970), 11-51; Jürgen Moltmann, "Covenant oder Leviathan? Zur Politischen Theologie der Neuzeit," *Zeitschrift für Theologie und Kirche* 90 (1993): 299-317.

37. Stephen Toulmin, *Cosmopolis: The Hidden Agenda of Modernity* (New York: The Free Press, 1990), 175ff.

38. Toulmin, *Cosmopolis*, 176.

39. Robert Darton, cited by Toulmin, *Cosmopolis*, 175-76.

But the notion of "the clean slate" has proven a dangerous myth. During the French Revolution and in particular later in the twentieth century we have learned by bitter experience that the slate cannot be cleaned and that in the process of trying to clean it a good deal of new dirt is generated — in fact, rivers of blood and mountains of corpses. Those lessons of history make us wonder whether some wisdom, in addition to accommodation, may be contained in 1 Peter's failure to challenge the oppressive structures of his day. What we should learn from the text is not, of course, to keep our mouths shut and hands folded, but to make our rhetoric and action more modest and more aligned with Christ's commands and example so that they can be more effective. As we strive for social change, 1 Peter nudges us to drop the pen that scripts master narratives and instead give account of the living hope in God and God's future (3:15; 1:5),[40] to abandon the project of reshaping society from the ground up and instead do as much good — personal and systemic — as we can from where we are at the time we are there (2:11), to suffer injustice and bless the unjust rather than perpetrating violence by repaying "evil for evil or abuse for abuse" (3:9), and to replace the anger of frustration with the joy of expectation (4:13).

Soft Difference

Though 1 Peter does not envisage changing social structures, Christians nevertheless have a mission in the world. They should conduct themselves "honorably among the Gentiles . . . so that they may see your honorable deeds and glorify God when he comes to judge" (2:12; cf. 3:1f.). Indeed, the purpose of Christian existence as a whole is to "proclaim the mighty acts of him who called you out of darkness into his marvelous light" (2:9). The distance from society that comes from the new birth into a living hope does not isolate from society. For hope in God, the creator and Savior of the whole world, knows no boundaries. Instead of leading

40. For a postmodern critique of master narratives see Jean-François Lyotard, *The Postmodern Condition: A Report on Knowledge* (trans. G. Bennington and B. Massumi; Minneapolis: University of Minnesota Press, 1984), 31ff. I am more persuaded by his critique than by his proposal, however.

to isolation, this distance is a presupposition of mission. Without distance, churches can only give speeches that others have written for them and only go places where others lead them. To make a difference, one must be different.[41]

The key question is how churches should think and live out their difference and their mission — both inalienable and mutually dependent dimensions of their identity. In one of the central passages in 1 Peter about the mission of the church, we come across a word that has today fallen somewhat into disrepute — the word "gentleness" or "meekness" (3:16; 3:4). As is well known, a certain kind of meekness is a weapon of the weak. They get their way by avoiding direct confrontations and by seemingly going with the flow. One might be tempted to interpret "gentleness" in 1 Peter as a debasing strategy of the powerless — i.e., be gentle, because being gentle is the only way to achieve what you desire in a hostile world.

One can only strike the enemy with the weapon of meekness, however, if one holds in the other hand a weapon called *guile.* This weapon is precisely the one 1 Peter takes out of the hands of his community (2:1f., 22). In place of guile, which tries to confuse the enemy by pretext (2:16), 1 Peter calls for the transparency of a pure heart (1:22). A gentleness that refuses to help itself with guile is no strategy of the weak. It is the open life-stance of the strong, who feel no need to support their own fragility by aggression toward others. Gentleness is the flipside of respect for the other. It is not an accident that gentleness and respect are mentioned together in 3:16, where Christians are told to give an account of the hope that is in them "with gentleness and reverence."[42]

It might be appropriate to call the missionary distance that 1 Peter stresses a *soft difference.* I do not mean a *weak* difference, for in 1 Peter

41. From the principle "no mission without difference" does not follow the quantitative principle "the bigger the difference, the more effective mission will be" (so K. H. Schelkle, *Die Petrusbriefe. Der Judasbrief* [HThK XIII/2; Freiburg: Herder, 1961], 72).

42. Goppelt (*Der erste Petrusbrief,* 237) suggests that *phobos* in 3:16 refers to fear before God and points to other instances in which the word is used with this meaning in 1 Peter (1:17; 2:18; 3:2). Even if one follows his interpretation in these other instances (as I think one should), the context in 3:16 points clearly toward respect for other people rather than reverence before God (see Brox, *Der erste Petrusbrief,* 160).

the difference is anything but weak. It is strong, but it is not hard. Fear for oneself and one's identity creates hardness. The difference that joins itself with hardness always presents the other with a choice: either submit or be rejected, either "become like me or get away from me." In the mission to the world, hard difference operates with open or hidden pressures, manipulation, and threats. A decision for a soft difference, on the other hand, presupposes a fearlessness that 1 Peter repeatedly encourages his readers to assume (3:14; 3:6). People who are secure in themselves — more accurately, who are secure in their God — are able to live the soft difference without fear. They have no need either to subordinate or damn others, but can allow others space to be themselves. For people who live the soft difference, mission fundamentally takes the form of witness and invitation. They seek to win others without pressure or manipulation, sometimes even "without a word" (3:1).

Whether it takes place gently or not, colonization is colonization. So might Tzvetan Todorov react to the pursuit of mission through soft difference. "Is there not already a violence in the conviction that one possesses the truth oneself, whereas this is not the case for others?" he asks rhetorically, commenting on the missionary efforts of such a friend of the Indians as Las Casas.[43] Instead of asserting the universal truth, one should strive to make the otherness of others blossom. Yet even "heightening of the other's differences" must be "guided by an emancipatory praxis that keeps the other empowered to be other,"[44] as Mark Taylor puts it. But when we ask what actually keeps others empowered to be authentically themselves, judgments about truth and error, freedom and slavery, darkness and light rush in. For unless you are willing to tolerate everything except intolerance toward everything, any notion of "emancipative praxis that keeps the other empowered to be other" involves often abstracting an authentic other from a concrete other and then affirming your abstraction while condemning the concrete other. You must abstract, for instance, from the fact that women are circumcised in a given culture before you can affirm that culture. But when you

43. Tzvetan Todorov, *The Conquest of America: The Question of the Other* (trans. R. Howard; New York: Harper Perennial, 1984), 168.

44. Mark Kline Taylor, "Religion, Cultural Plurality, and Liberating Praxis: In Conversation with the Work of Langdon Gilkey," *Journal of Religion* 71/2 (1992): 162.

affirm the other in this way, you have not affirmed them, but your own construction of their authentic identity, a construction that entails making judgments about truth and value. And so we are back at proclaiming the truth that others do not possess. The difference is that we now do it clandestinely, whereas 1 Peter would want us to do it openly. Truth will be spoken, value judgments will be made. The question is only how — upfront or surreptitiously, with harshness or with gentleness, from a position of power or from a position of "weakness."

Just as gentleness is not a mere survival strategy, so the soft difference is not simply a missionary method. Rather, the soft difference is the missionary side of following in the footsteps of the crucified Messiah. It is not an optional extra, but part and parcel of Christian identity itself. To be a Christian means to live one's own identity in the face of others in such a way that one joins inseparably the belief in the truth of one's own convictions with a respect for the convictions of others. The softness that should characterize the very being of Christians — I am tempted to call it "ontic gentleness" — must not be given up even when we are (from our own perspective) persuaded that others are either wrong or evil. To give up the softness of our difference would be to sacrifice our identity as followers of Jesus Christ.

Difference and Commensurability

One is immediately struck in 1 Peter with two contrary reactions of outsiders to the soft missionary difference. On the one hand, there is angered surprise and blaspheming from non-Christians that Christians are no longer joining them "in the same excesses of dissipation" (4:4). The Christian difference is the cause of discrimination and persecution. Moreover, 1 Peter tells us, such negative reaction is to be expected from non-Christians. Christians should not be surprised by the "fiery ordeal" they have to endure (4:12). The negative reactions of non-Christians do not rest on misunderstanding but are rooted in the inner logic of the constellation of values of some in the surrounding culture that seem incompatible with the values of Christians. On the other hand, one of the central passages in 1 Peter entertains a lively hope that precisely the

Christian difference — outwardly visible in their good deeds — will cause non-Christians to see the truth and eventually convert (2:12, 15; 3:1, 16). This expectation presupposes overlap between Christian and non-Christian constellations of values. The good works of Christians can be appreciated by non-Christians and look attractive to them.

Commensurability and incommensurability between Christian and non-Christian value patterns are so intertwined in 1 Peter that they can appear in one and the same sentence: "Conduct yourself honorably among the Gentiles, so that, through that for which they malign you as evildoers, they may see your honorable deeds and glorify God when he comes to judge" (2:12). The very actions the Gentiles malign as evil deeds will ultimately be recognized by them as good deeds if Christians do consistently what non-Christians malign. Non-Christians will even convert on account of these good deeds. Two seemingly contradictory reactions exist side by side! Can one reconcile them?

One way to resolve the problem is to invoke the miracle of *seeing*. Non-Christians look at the same phenomenon, but they are no longer provoked to anger because they come to it from a different perspective — the perspective of faith. Yet the miracle of seeing can happen only when one has already come to faith.[45] Consequently, coming to faith would not be the result of observing good works, but perceiving good works would be the result of coming to faith. Moreover, the presupposition of this solution is that value patterns of Christians and non-Christians are incommensurable. There are no bridges or overlaps. The only thing one can do is jump from one value system into another for no apparent reason or, possibly, out of dissatisfaction. But what is significant in 1 Peter is that commensurability and incommensurability are taking place at one and the same time, that good works themselves are both the cause of blaspheming (4:4) and the cause for glorifying God (2:12).[46] How is this possible?

---

45. So rightly from his perspective Goppelt, *Der erste Petrusbrief,* 160.

46. It could be suggested that we try to resolve the tension between angered surprise and the embracing of Christian faith by appealing to the passage of time. At first the Gentiles are angry, and then, after longer observation of honorable Christian living, they have to admit their error. If the tension could be resolved in this way, however, Christians could not see discrimination and persecution as something natural; they

The stress on Christian difference notwithstanding, the "world" does not seem a monolithic place in 1 Peter. We encounter evil people who persecute Christians and who will continue to do the same by blaspheming what is most holy to Christians (4:4, 12). We come across ignorant and foolish people who will be silenced by Christian good behavior (2:15). We meet people who know what is wrong and what is right and are ready to relate to Christians accordingly (2:14). Finally, we encounter people who see, appreciate, and are finally won over to the Christian faith (2:12; 3:1).[47] Thus the picture is more complex than just the two extreme and contrary reactions. This testifies to a sensitivity in 1 Peter to the complexity of the social environment.

Let me try to explicate the implicit understanding of the social world. The world consists of a plurality of "worlds." The values of these worlds do not form tight and comprehensive systems; they are not like balls that touch but do not connect. Rather, each of these worlds consists of a mixture of partly self-consistent and partly disparate practices and thought patterns. In addition, the worlds are in a permanent social interchange which shapes values that are partly common to the interacting social worlds, partly merely compatible, and partly contrary. An essential dimension of the interchange is the struggle for social power. In this struggle, ethical persuasions and various interests collide, not only between various parties, but also within one party or even within a single person. Jean-François Lyotard paints an extreme version of a similar picture when he writes:

> The social subject itself seems to dissolve in this dissemination of language games. The social bond is linguistic, but is not woven with a single thread. It is a fabric formed by the intersection of at least two (and in reality an indeterminate number) of language games, obeying different rules.[48]

---

would have to be surprised at its persistence. But according to 1 Peter Christians should consider persecution natural (see 4:12).

47. Elliott seems to want to harmonize all these reactions and ascribe them to non-Christians monolithically understood (see "1 Peter, Its Situation and Strategy," 69).

48. Lyotard, *The Postmodern Condition,* 40.

If we do not take too seriously the talk about the dissolution of the subject,[49] Lyotard's description of the complex social interaction seems right on target.

Notice the consequences of such a picture of the social world for the question of commensurability between value systems of discrete social groups (such as a Christian church). In such a world, one cannot speak either of the principled commensurability or of the principled incommensurability of value systems. Of course, one can imagine situations in which value systems of communities *are* fully commensurable or are completely incommensurable. But this image is theory, not reality. As a rule, however, communities' value systems are partly commensurable and partly incommensurable. They can even be commensurable and incommensurable at the same time, insofar as the values within one community or within one single person can be contradictory. Thus when we find commensurability and incommensurability at one and the same time in 1 Peter, we should not be too quick to accuse 1 Peter of inconsistency, but rather ask whether our urge for consistency does not skew our perception of social reality. The epistle shows remarkable and refreshing sensibility for the complexity of social realities; it bursts a way of thinking that operates with stark polarities.

In addition to explaining the different ways in which non-Christians relate to the gospel, the complex interplay of commensurability and incommensurability suggests also that there is no single proper way for Christians to relate to a given culture as a whole. Instead, there are numerous ways of accepting, rejecting, subverting, or transforming various aspects of a culture which is itself a complex pattern of symbols, beliefs, values, practices, and organizations that are partly congruent with one another and partly contradictory. It seems obvious, but is in no way trite, to note that 1 Peter does not speak abstractly about the relation between gospel and culture. Much like other New Testament writings, the epistle does not deal explicitly with "culture" as the place of Christian presence, nor with "society" as a field of Christian responsibility.[50] But it does pro-

49. For a critique of the postmodern dissolution of the subject see Alasdair MacIntyre, *Three Rival Versions of Moral Enquiry: Encyclopaedia, Genealogy, and Tradition* (Notre Dame: University of Notre Dame Press, 1990), 196ff.

50. So rightly Brox, *Der erste Petrusbrief,* 18.

vide some overarching perspectives about how particular Christians in Asia Minor at a particular time should relate to their diverse neighbors. Even if we find abstractions necessary and models of relating to a culture useful, we should not lose sight of the rich diversity within any given culture and therefore of the multiple ways in which the gospel relates to it, such as being "against the culture" and "converting the culture," "subverting the culture" and in some sense being even "of the culture" — all at the same time.

Church, Sect, or Something Else?

After the foregoing exegetical and theological analysis of Christian identity and difference in 1 Peter, let us revisit in our conclusion the church-sect typology and ask about the nature of the Petrine community as it is portrayed in 1 Peter. It seems that, through the new birth into a living hope, a "sect" was born. And indeed, before the newborn child could take her first breath, her difference, her foreignness, was manifest. As she was growing up, there was no question that she did not quite fit into her environment.

Soon, however, she began to confuse observers by provoking uncertainty about her sectarian identity. It looked as though she did not forge her identity through rejection of her social environment, but through the acceptance of God's gift of salvation and its values. She refused to operate within the alternative "affirmation of the world" versus "denial of the world," but surprised people with strange combinations of difference and acculturation. She was sure of her mission to proclaim the mighty deeds of God for the salvation of the world, but refused to use either pressure or manipulation. Rather, she lived fearlessly her soft difference. She was not surprised by the various reactions of individuals and communities among whom she lived, because she was aware of the bewildering complexity of social worlds in which values are partly the same, partly different, sometimes complementary, and sometimes contradictory. And so it gradually became clear that the child who was born again through the resurrection of Jesus Christ from the dead into a living hope was not a sect at all. The unusual child who looked like a sect, but did not act like a sect, was a Christian community — a church that can serve as a model even for us today as we reflect on the nature of Christian presence in modern, rapidly changing, pluralistic societies that resist being shaped by moral norms.

CHAPTER FOUR

Peculiar Politics: John's Gospel, Dualism, and Contemporary Pluralism

———— ✸✸✸ ————

What's fascinating about the topic of Johannine dualism and contemporary pluralism is that it trades on two longstanding if somewhat vague assumptions. The first is that John's Gospel — indeed the Johannine corpus as a whole — advocates a stark form of religious dualism, whereas cultural pluralism is an important feature of the contemporary world. St. John's and today's world are at odds with each other. John knows only of negatively coded darkness and positively coded light with nothing in between. The first he identifies with "this world" and "below," the second with the "heavenly world" and "above." Today's world, in contrast, is a world of many colors, and all of them are deemed beautiful, singly and together. Moreover, for many of our contemporaries, the world above is an impossibility; in modernity it seems a

I want to thank the participants of the conference on "St. John and Theology" at the University of St. Andrews (especially professors Steven Barton, Richard Bauckham, Judith Lieu, Andrew Lincoln, Marianne Meye Thompson, Steve Motyer, and Alan Torrance), where a shorter version of this essay was originally presented, as well as my friends and colleagues at Yale — Shane Berg and professors Harold Attridge, Adela Collins, and Wayne Meeks — for critically engaging a draft of this essay. I owe special thanks to Professor Robert H. Gundry with whom I extensively discussed — indeed, debated in a friendly manner — the ideas contained in the essay and who offered detailed comments on both its substance and its style.

given, as Peter Sloterdijk has put it, that "nothing but the world may be the case."[1] The second persuasion is that pluralism is good and dualism bad, bad in the intellectual sense of being just plain mistaken, as representing an illicit reduction of the world's complexity. Dualism is also seen as bad in the moral sense of always creating ill; it suppresses legitimate plurality by seeking to shape it according to a series of binary opposites. Pluralism, on the other hand, is good because it respects the world's complexity, in that it both recognizes its existence and affirms it as a positive good.

The two assumptions together amount to an implicit claim that John's Gospel is not only unsaintly but positively harmful in today's world. I am not aware that anyone has written a critique of John's Gospel comparable to Friedrich Nietzsche's vitriol against Paul in *Anti-Christ*[2] or to Gilles Deleuze's decrying the violence of John of Patmos in "Nietzsche and Paul, Lawrence and John of Patmos."[3] But given how influential John's Gospel was and remains — just think of the millions of booklets containing John's Gospel that have been distributed in the past few decades in an attempt to evangelize the world! — and how much at odds it is perceived to be with contemporary cultural sensibilities, I am surprised that it has not been targeted for a scathing critique. A critic of John would castigate him less for hostility to life (as in Nietzsche's critique of Paul as a theologian of *ressentiment*) or for wreaking religious violence on enemies (as in Deleuze's critique of John of Patmos as a theologian with a dagger between his teeth) and more for lumping together all the world's diversity and consigning it to the realm of darkness and hatred under the rule of Satan so as to construe himself and his community as a realm of light and love under the rule of God. Was this massive act of exclusion at the heart of John's thought not as problematic as Paul's "hatred"? And John of Patmos was honest enough to advocate violence openly, whereas John the Evangelist hid his exclusion under the guise of self-giving love.

1. Peter Sloterdijk, *Weltfremdheit* (Frankfurt a.M.: Suhrkamp, 1993), 106. He uses the phrase "wittgensteinian in origin" to describe modernity.

2. Friedrich Nietzsche, *Twilight of the Idols and Anti-Christ* (trans. R. J. Hollingdale; London: Penguin, 1990).

3. Gilles Deleuze, *Kleine Schriften* (trans. K. D. Schacht; Berlin: Minerva, 1980).

From afar, this picture is indeed how John may appear to the modern reader: not saintly but beastly. Though I have not studied the history of the Gospel's reception, I would be surprised if his sharp dualities have not been used to give religious sanction to what are nothing but acts of exclusion. Yet the closer we get to John, the less persuasive such a reading of him becomes — or so I will argue in this essay. First, I will show that John's Gospel is not dualistic and that the oppositional dualities that we actually do find in it may be more salutary than the facile celebration of plurality characteristic of contemporary culture — indeed more salutary for, among other things, the flourishing of plurality itself. Second, I will explore the extent to which there are shades of gray and not just radical contrasts on either side of John's oppositional dualities. Within the positive ends of those dualities, I will pay special attention to the fate of plurality.

I should state at the outset that for the purposes of this essay "Johannine" will mainly refer to the thought of John's Gospel. I will read the Gospel as a finished product without inquiring historically into the origins of the Johannine community or life situation at the time the Gospel was written, let alone examining the Gospel's relation to what Jesus was originally all about. Also I will not distinguish what the Evangelist may have originally written from what a redactor or other minor contributors may have added. Such inquiries and distinctions involve reconstructions that strike me, a theologian and not an exegete or a historian, as too conjectural and circular to be of much theological or broader intellectual value. I will engage the text as we have it preserved, not completely unlike the way a contemporary philosopher might interpret a text of Plato or Descartes. There is nothing in this approach, of course, that requires us to treat John merely as a "chapter in the history of ideas" without attending to how these ideas function in a given social setting. I am interested both in John's ideas and in their function — the ideas contained in the finished text and their function in various social contexts.

Methodologically, the decision to treat the text as an integral whole is momentous. It makes the interpretative task possibly less involved, hopefully more profitable, but likely more difficult. Why more difficult? Obvious tensions in the Gospel, and there are many, can be easily solved by multiplying authors and life situations in which they wrote and by explaining that these discrete parts were only later stitched together into the text we have presently. For instance, those who see a tension or even a contradiction between the universalistic claim that the Word is "the true light, which enlightens everyone" (1:9) and a particularistic claim of Jesus that he is "the way, and the truth, and the life" (14:6), or between the affirmation that "God . . . loved the world" (3:16) and Jesus' statement that he "does not pray for the world" (17:9), can assign different statements to different authors and end up with neat positions. But quite apart from the procedure's being conjectural and circular, it is more or less, well, *boring:* The interpreter ends up with a smart book of historical reconstructions containing a string of flat positions.[4] It is religiously and intellectually more profitable to explore the rich relief of the existent text, even if we occasionally have to build bridges across canyons and dig tunnels under impassable mountains.

Dualism

What is religious dualism? What is contemporary pluralism? How does John relate to both? I will speak briefly on dualism; pluralism and John's relation to it I will engage more extensively.

As is well known, "dualism" has become a convenient term of opprobrium. A duality deemed unacceptable is rejected as dualistic. Such

---

4. The methodological decision to read the Gospel from the perspective of what is considered characteristic and unique has, on the whole, the same flattening effect. One construes the theology of John from what is deemed characteristic, and leaves behind other things as irrelevant — things that are said to trail along without being an organic part of John's theology — as though one were making a map of a mountainous region from an airplane on a cloudy day and noting only peaks but nothing below them. It is possible to chop off the peaks, so to speak, for apologetic reasons (Ernst Käsemann, *The Testament of Jesus: A Study of the Gospel of John in the Light of Chapter 17* [trans. Gerhard Krodel; Philadelphia: Fortress, 1968], 28). But it is no less problematic to disregard everything *but* peaks in a misplaced zeal for the unique. John can be understood adequately only by holding together the characteristic and the common even when there is a strong tension between them. It is the potentially tension-filled combination of both that gives the Gospel of John — and any other writing, indeed any other thing — its peculiar character.

empty notions of dualism, which allow it to stand for any unacceptable duality, tell us much about the position of the person using the term but little about dualism itself. A more substantive notion of dualism is necessary. Ugo Bianchi offers a compelling one when he writes,

> As a category within the history and phenomenology of religion, dualism may be defined as a doctrine that posits the existence of two fundamental causal principles underlying the existence . . . of the world. In addition, dualistic doctrines, worldviews, or myths represent the basic components of the world or of man as participating in the ontological opposition and disparity of value that characterize their dual principles.[5]

Two observations are worth making about Bianchi's definition. First, *metaphysical irreducibility,* as in Descartes' substantial distinction between *res cogitans* and *res extensa,* is not in itself sufficient to make a position dualistic. For it may well be that a single divine being is the origin of both metaphysically irreducible components of reality. Second, strict *moral opposition* between good and evil as well as between their respective protagonists is as such not dualistic. "The simple contrasting of good and evil, life and death, light and darkness, and so on is in fact coextensive with religion itself and cannot be equated with the much more specific phenomenon of dualism,"[6] argues Bianchi. We speak properly of dualism only when such dualities are connected with the opposite ontological "principles responsible for bringing the world and man into existence."[7]

If we accept Bianchi's definition of dualism, John's Gospel is clearly not a dualistic document. True, stable and firm oppositional dualities structure the text: above and below, heavenly realm and world, light and darkness, spirit and flesh, good and evil, truth and falsehood, God and the devil, children of God and children of the devil. And yet none of these dualities, singly or together, imply dualism.

First, John's Gospel starts with the affirmation that God through the

---

5. Ugo Bianchi, "Dualism," in *Encyclopedia of Religion,* vol. 4 (ed. Mircea Eliade; New York: Macmillan, 1987), 506.

6. Bianchi, "Dualism," 506.

7. Bianchi, "Dualism," 506.

Word *created* everything that is not divine (1:3). As a consequence, the creation as a whole can be properly described as "what is his [the Word's] own" (1:10). All the oppositional dualities within creation and between creation and God exist ultimately on account of God's creative activity. Did God then create "the darkness" (1:5) into which the light of the Word is shining (much as the Qumran community believed that God "appointed two spirits for him [man] in which to walk until the time of His visitation: the spirit of truth and falsehood" [1QS 3.17-18])? Ernst Käsemann thought so. He argued that John's dualism is neither "metaphysical dualism" nor "dualism of decision" (i.e., dualism effected by human decision[8]) but a dualism of "the effect of the Word"[9] — the Word creates cosmos and chaos, light and darkness. But this position cannot be correct. The light along with life is "in" the Word (1:4) and is therefore a primordial reality that precedes creation and is a condition of its possibility, not simply one element in it. Darkness is the creature's self-contradictory shutting-of-itself-from-the-light[10] and is by no means the effect of the Word. Instead of creating darkness, the light dispels it. Wisely, John leaves the existence of darkness unexplained. But if darkness was not created by God yet still somehow exists, are we back to metaphysical dualism? No, because *all* things were created by God and therefore darkness can be only "no-thing," a negation of an original and originally good creation.

Second, God is not only the creator but also the *redeemer* of creation. The aim of God's redemptive activity is to overcome oppositional duali-

---

8. See Rudolf Bultmann, *Theology of the New Testament*, vol. 2 (trans. Kendrick Grobel; New York: Charles Scribner, 1955), 21, 76.

9. Käsemann, *The Testament of Jesus*, 63.

10. For Augustine, "darkness" in John is both the inability to perceive light on account of sin and the resultant state of the sinner. Commenting on John 1, he writes, "But, it may be, the dull hearts of some cannot yet receive this light. Their sins weigh them down, and they cannot discern it. Let them not think, however, that, because they cannot discern it, therefore it is not present with them. For they themselves, because of their sins, are darkness; *and the light shineth in darkness, and the darkness comprehendeth it not.* . . . If a man were unable to see by reason of dust, or water, or smoke which had got into his eyes, and injured them, his surgeon would say to him, 'Wipe from your eye whatever hurts it, that you may be able to see the light of your eyes'" (Augustine, *Homilies on the Gospel According to St. John and His First Epistle*, vol. 1 [Oxford: John Henry Parker, 1848], 17).

ties — darkness versus light, below versus above, falsehood versus truth — so as to leave room in creation only for reconciled differences. By becoming flesh, the Word intimately united itself precisely to that which has alienated itself from God (1:14). Moreover, God loved the world that was opposed to him (3:16); and the incarnate Word became "the Lamb of God who takes away the sin of the world" (1:29). The result is at least the partial transformation of oppositional dualities into non-oppositional ones: duality between God and world is transformed into communion between God and Jesus' disciples. As a consequence, oppositional dualities within the creation are overcome too: enmity between men and women is overcome in a community of equality among them,[11] ethnic divisions between Jews and Samaritans, between Jews and Greeks, are bridged in a single community that worships God "in spirit and truth" (4:23). John's accounts of creation and redemption together undercut dualistic modes of thought. As Rudolf Bultmann correctly observed, cosmological dualism is overcome "in the fact that by [John] the world continues to be understood as God's creation and in the fact that [his] God-concept . . . contains the paradoxical notion of judgment and grace."[12]

We could object that the tracing of everything that is non-God back to God happens only in the Prologue, which stands in an uneasy relation to the rest of the Gospel. Though I cannot enter here into the debate over whether there is in fact a tension between the Prologue and the rest of the Gospel, it seems clear that God's redemptive activity depends on God's creative activity. For John, God's love for the world, which leads to its salvation — the two themes emphasized outside the Prologue — makes sense against the backdrop of the world belonging to God as God's creation.

Another possible objection could go something like this: The declarations of God's loving the world and the Lamb's saving the world notwithstanding, the oppositional duality between the world and God, along with all other derivative dualities, increases rather than lessens as the story progresses. But the increasing of oppositional dualities can be

11. It is generally recognized that when it comes to relations between men and women, John is the most egalitarian of all New Testament writings (see Käsemann, *The Testament of Jesus*, 31).

12. Bultmann, *Theology of the New Testament*, 2:10.

read either as their confirmation or as a precondition of their being over-come. The latter is the case in John. An increase in tension is exactly what we should expect, especially if redemption is to happen through the *death* of the Lamb. The apparent obliteration of good by evil is the way in which evil is overcome by the enactment of divine goodness. The very opposite of dualism is at work here. God, who is love, loves the es-tranged world to the point of assuming flesh in order to suffer death at the hands of the world. In this way God not only opens the road for the world's return but also attracts it back to himself. God loves first and en-acts this love on the cross so that human beings may love God and God's creatures in return (cf. 1 John 3:8-10).

Even if John is not ultimately dualistic, he makes some of the most rigid oppositional dualities of any New Testament writer. The problem of John's relation to pluralism has been altered but not eliminated by the re-jection of dualistic readings of his Gospel. But how we understand and address the problem will depend on our notions of pluralism.

Pluralism as a Political Project

We use "pluralism" today in three related yet logically independent ways: (1) pluralism as a social fact; (2) pluralism as a philosophical stance; (3) pluralism as a political project. Given my contention that John is not dualistic but instead operates with oppositional dualities, the question I am pursuing must be rephrased: What is the relation between Johannine oppositional dualities and these three forms of pluralism? Let me begin with the last form.

Pluralism as a *political project* is an attempt to construct the kinds of political arrangements best suited for culturally and religiously pluralistic societies. Nicholas Wolterstorff, a philosopher with a Christian political vision, has suggested a form of such political arrangements: a pluralistic liberal democracy. Two features distinguish it from other conceptions of liberal democracy, notably from that of John Rawls.[13] First, it dispenses

---

13. See John Rawls, *Theory of Justice* (Cambridge, Mass.: Harvard University Press, 1971); John Rawls, *Political Liberalism* (New York: Columbia University Press, 1993).

with the notion of a shared political basis rooted in the idea of public reason. Instead, argues Wolterstorff, we should learn to live "with the politics of multiple communities."[14] Second, the state should be "neutral with respect to the religious and other comprehensive perspectives present in society," and the state's neutrality should be understood "as requiring *impartiality* of the state with respect to all comprehensive perspectives rather than *separation* of the state from all of them."[15] Such a notion of liberal democracy, which presumes neither a single public reason nor a state that promotes none of the goods of particular communities, is one way — one good way, I would argue together with Wolterstorff — to pursue genuinely pluralistic political arrangements.

John's oppositional dualities have virtually nothing to do with pluralism as a political project. First, nothing in the notion of pluralism as a political project excludes communities that operate with strong oppositional dualities, such as between a holy church and a sinful world, good and evil, God and the devil; it does not even exclude communities with strictly dualistic worldviews. To the contrary, the point of this form of pluralism is to accommodate *on an equal footing* various communities that may operate with such oppositional dualities as well as those — still a minority — that do not. The community of the beloved disciple with its lives, loves, and hates (to use the description of Raymond Brown[16]) would be simply one of the many communities in a larger polity not only allowed but even *encouraged* to pursue its own comprehensive perspective on life.

Second, nothing in the life perspective of a Johannine-like community speaks against pluralism as a political project. Its pervasive oppositional dualities would lie on a different plane from that of political arrangements. True, its relatively sharp line of demarcation between the community of believers and the world of unbelievers — a line, as we will

14. Nicholas Wolterstorff, "The Role of Religion in Decision and Discussion of Political Issues," in *Religion in the Public Square: The Place of Religious Convictions in Political Debate* (ed. Robert Audi and Nicholas Wolterstorff; Lanham, Md.: Rowman & Littlefield, 1997), 109.

15. Wolterstorff, "The Role of Religion," 115.

16. See Raymond E. Brown, *The Community of the Beloved Disciple: The Lives, Loves, and Hates of an Individual Church in New Testament Times* (New York: Paulist, 1979).

see below, that in John ends up strangely blurry — as well as its orientation away from an earthly to a heavenly realm, would tend to discourage its members from actively promoting pluralistic political arrangements. But the community would no more reject such arrangements than it would any other political arrangement, whether nonpluralistic liberal democracy, authoritarian socialism, or Roman imperialism. And if such a community saw itself as countercultural (as the Johannine community did), we could see how, under different circumstances from those of Greco-Roman antiquity, the community might have had some stake in preferring political arrangements that allowed it to exist on equal footing with other communities, however different from — and, from a religious standpoint, incompatible with — its own.[17] For pluralistic political arrangements would have allowed it to flourish as a counterculture. Such a community could have lived happily with pluralism as a political project and may even have had internal reasons to prefer it to available alternatives.

Pluralism as a Philosophical Stance

What is the relation of John's Gospel to pluralism as a *philosophical stance?* In his book *Pluralism: Against the Demand of Consensus,* Nicholas Rescher has suggested that pluralism as a philosophical stance comes in four basic versions: (1) *skepticism,* according to which no single position is justified and all alternatives simply cancel each other out; (2) *syncretism,* according to which all alternatives should be accepted as justified and

17. Oppositional dualities mark John as belonging loosely to the type of Christian community Max Weber, and after him Ernst Troeltsch, have described with the term "sect." It is important to note that the Western idea of toleration emerged from within the sectarian mentality, with its oppositional dualities. As Troeltsch has shown, this almost paradoxical fact has to do with sects' understandable renunciation of coercion in matters of religion (Ernst Troeltsch, *The Social Teaching of the Christian Churches* [New York: Harper, 1960], 995). As I will argue below, it is not quite correct in either the theological or sociological sense to describe the Johannine community as a sect. But still, it shares with the ideal-type sect the endorsement of oppositional dualities (carefully qualified), and as in the case of sects, these dualities would not prevent but in fact would put some pressure on it to endorse pluralism as a political project.

somehow conjoined and juxtaposed; (3) *indifferentist relativism,* according to which "only one alternative should be accepted, but this acceptance cannot be based on rationally cogent grounds but emerges from considerations that themselves lack any rational basis — as a matter of taste, of 'personal inclination', or social tradition, or some such"; (4) *contextualism,* according to which "only one alternative should be accepted, and this acceptance has a basis of rational cogency, albeit this basis may differ perspectivally from group to group, era to era, and school to school."[18]

Clearly, none of these options would be acceptable from the perspective of John's Gospel. The Word is the "true light, which enlightens everyone" (1:9); the Word-become-flesh, who is none other than the Father's only Son, is "full of grace and truth" (1:14); Jesus is "the truth" (14:7) and, before Pilate, declares, "For this I was born, and for this I came into the world, to testify to the truth" (18:37). Jesus' disciples too can be confident of knowing the truth; the "Spirit of truth" will guide them into "all the truth" (14:17; 15:26; 16:13). In John, it is not Jesus or his disciples who are disdainful of the talk about truth and instead interested in relations of power, but a Roman ruler who condemns the innocent Jesus to be crucified (18:38).

Not that John is unaware of the situated character of human knowledge — the fact that we are not suspended above the plurality that marks our world, as though by some sky hook, as we seek to know. For John, truth is not a ripe fruit to be plucked by any passerby or even only by those with tools to reach it. A person will come to light and know the truth only if she "*does* what is true" (3:21); she has to "*belong* to the truth" to recognize the truth of Jesus' words (18:37). Truthful knowing is situated in the sense that it depends partly on the moral character of the knower, which in turn depends partly on her allegiances and on the community to which she belongs.[19] A person's *affinity* with the truth is a con-

18. Nicholas Rescher, *Pluralism: Against the Demand of Consensus* (Oxford: Clarendon, 1993), 80.

19. As far as I can tell, John has nothing to say about the kinds of epistemological questions that many philosophers like to discuss, such as whether the thing lying on the mat is a dog or a cat or whether the perceptions we have somehow do or do not track with the actual character of the world (see, for instance, Bertrand Russell, *The*

dition for the recognition of the truth.[20] And yet the truth is one and not many, absolute and not relative, transcendent and not immanent. In John's account, truth does not depend on personal inclination or differ from group to group; human *knowledge* of the truth does. Even with Jesus as "the truth" before them (14:6), the disciples still need to be led into all truth (16:13)!

It is not clear, however, that the incompatibility of John's Gospel with pluralism as a philosophical stance is to John's, rather than pluralism's, discredit. All versions of pluralism as a philosophical stance are open to serious criticisms. Rescher has plausibly argued against the first three. *Skeptical* pluralism claims that alternative positions cancel each other and that therefore none should be embraced. But why would they cancel each other? The belief that they do presumes that "where different individuals or groups opt for different alternatives, they do so with equal justification."[21] There are no indications that this presumption is in fact true. *Syncretistic* pluralism claims that all alternatives are equally true, a position that becomes self-defeating: "It cannot avoid seeing the alternatives to itself (skepticism, absolutism, etc.) as equally valid. In being embracing it renders itself declaratively empty."[22] *Relativist* pluralism makes all stances into consequences of tastes and preferences. Hence it is unable to make any rationally cogent claim or contention, including that of relativism,[23] and transmutes all disputes into relations of power.

Contextual pluralism, Rescher's own version, fares no better than the alternatives he critiques. Rescher wants to have his cake and eat it, too.

Problems of Philosophy [Indianapolis: Hackett, 2000], 7-59). Most of John's talk about truth is religious. Could he have accepted the importance of contextual factors in ordinary acts of knowledge in analogy to his recognition of the importance of a knower's character for adequate knowing in the religious realm? There is simply no way to tell, though I do not see anything in the structure of his thought that would prevent him from doing so.

20. For my argument here, it does not matter precisely how this affinity is accomplished. It may simply be a humanly willed affinity, a result of God's elective purposes (6:44; 15:16), or, most likely in John, both. My point is simply to underscore the necessity of affinity *with* the truth for recognition *of* the truth.

21. Rescher, *Pluralism*, 88.

22. Rescher, *Pluralism*, 94.

23. Rescher, *Pluralism*, 104.

To be contextual, valid justifications for positions are necessarily dependent on the context, and yet to be pluralistic, alternative philosophical positions must enjoy "a parity of status from an *external* point of view."[24] The external point of view that would allow one to show a parity of status of positions must be an overarching perspective outside any particular one. The problem is that, given his affirmation of contextualism, no such external point of view is available. He must give up on either contextualism or pluralism.

In short, pluralism as a philosophical stance is implausible. Affirmation of oppositional duality in matters of truth and value — truth versus falsehood and good versus evil — seems to be the only viable way to proceed. This is especially the case for theologians who, like me, advocate a near-classical account of God. Affirmation of oppositional duality between truth and falsehood and good and evil, moreover, may be the best way to preserve social pluralism and make it flourish — or so I shall argue in the following section. My arguments against pluralism as a philosophical stance and for oppositional dualities in matters of truth and value in and of themselves in no way imply, of course, that John's *beliefs* about what is true and good are correct. All that these arguments show is that he is right to operate with oppositional dualities in matters of truth and value, which is to say that his allegedly dualistic mode of thought is not a problem, but an asset.

Pluralism as a Social Phenomenon

By "pluralism as a social phenomenon," I mean simply the fact of cultural diversity in the world today. To say that our world is culturally pluralistic in this third sense is not so much to prescribe how each culture should be evaluated (pluralism as a normative stance) and how they should relate to each other (pluralism as a political project) as to note that a plurality of cultures is a social reality.

It is sometimes claimed that the world has become increasingly pluralistic in this sense. If by "world" we mean the whole inhabited earth,

24. Rescher, *Pluralism*, 105.

this claim is manifestly not the case. To the contrary, in recent centuries, first through the creation of unified social spaces by nation-states and then by processes of globalization, beginning with colonization and extending all the way to their present post-colonial phase, we have witnessed a significant *reduction* of cultural plurality.[25] If by "world" we mean "Western countries," it is true that over the past decades some forms of cultural plurality have increased. Formerly "Christian nations" have become culturally and religiously pluralistic nations. We live near or with people whose mores, values, and overarching interpretations of life differ markedly from ours and who have sufficient social power to make their voices heard and their collective decisions felt in the public square.

Cultural plurality is a general term that encompasses significantly different ways in which those who are mutually "other" relate. "Others" may be simply *different* from us — say, by speaking Hungarian or Slovenian instead of Croatian or Italian. Or they may *disapprove* of some of the constitutive features of our otherness, such as our use of alcohol, if they happen to be Muslim, or the practice of genital mutilation, if we are members of a particular African tribe. Or others may be those who have *transgressed* against us as, most likely, we also did against them, as the Hutus who have massacred hundreds of thousands of Tutsis, and Catholics and Protestants who have killed each other in Ireland. Indeed, the other may, and often does, fit all three of these descriptions.

How are oppositional dualities in John related to pluralism as a social phenomenon? If "all things came into being through him [the Word], and without him not one thing came into being" (1:3), plurality as a social fact, along with plurality as a metaphysical fact, is not only obviously affirmed but is also traced back to God's creative activity. Without some form of plurality, there would be no things outside God, whether these things are individual creatures, males or females, or languages. And for

25. The fate of the world's languages is indicative of the reduction in cultural plurality. Linguistics experts estimate that of the world's approximately six thousand living languages, half are in danger of extinction. For an argument that globalization threatens linguistic diversity and therefore cultural plurality see Andrew Dalby, *Language in Danger: The Loss of Linguistic Diversity and the Threat to Our Future* (New York: Columbia University Press, 2003).

John, plurality of things is grounded in God and therefore implicitly affirmed as good. Far from entailing a denial of plurality, nonoppositional duality between God and creation is, according to John, a de facto precondition of there being any plurality of a natural or social kind, including a variety of inner-creaturely nonoppositional dualities, such as that between male and female.[26]

The matter is more complicated when it comes to oppositional dualities — truth versus falsehood, community of believers versus world, etc. In principle, oppositional dualities do not exclude plurality. Even if the truth is one, it may come in many versions, and falsehood is famously multiple. As we shall see, the community of believers is internally differentiated in John. With regard to unbelievers, there are many ways to be worldly, and those who are believers come in many shapes and colors and speak many languages. So talk of the evil and deceitful world clearly admits of plurality. Nevertheless, the point of oppositional dualities is to eliminate evil and falsehood and deny the normative legitimacy of all forms of worldliness. If John were to have his way, cultural forms would remain, but all people would align themselves with one truth, one goodness, and one God; the broad stream of the play of cultural difference would be channeled into the confines marked by truth and goodness as defined by the one God in his revealer, Jesus Christ. Is there then a tension between nonoppositional and oppositional dualities, the first establishing and affirming plurality and the second denying and seeking to overcome it — at least those forms of it that are not aligned with God, goodness, and truth? Or could it be that John's oppositional dualities stand in the service of a plurality which essentially characterizes God's creation?

Confrontation with "the Jews"

Take the infamous confrontation between Jesus and "the Jews" in John. The most extreme oppositional dualities anywhere in the Gospel, as well

---

26. My point here is not to claim that one needs to postulate God in order to have plurality, though such may well be the case, but that *for John* the existence of plurality is grounded in God.

as other, less stark oppositional dualities, are used in this confrontation: Jesus comes from above, from God; "the Jews" are from below, the children of the prince of this world. "You are from your father the devil, and you choose to do your father's desires," says John's Jesus. "He was a murderer from the beginning and does not stand in the truth, because there is no truth in him. When he lies, he speaks according to his own nature, for he is a liar and the father of lies" (8:44-45). This language seems dysphemistic at its extreme, a literal demonization of a whole people, the Jews. Do we have here oppositional dualism placed at the service of a most radical exclusion of at least one legitimate member of the existent social plurality, according to the Hebrew Scriptures, the chosen people of God? I don't think so — at least, not if we stay at the level of the interpretation of the Gospel's text.

First, Jesus' negative characterization of the Jews here *follows* their own description of him as demon possessed (7:20; 8:48, 52; 10:20) and, more importantly, their attempts to kill him (5:18; 7:1, 19, 25, 30; 8:37, 40; 11:53).[27] Prior to Jesus' healing of a man on the Sabbath, there are no negative designations of the Jews, only neutral or positive ones. All negative statements about "the Jews" are framed by their attempts to kill Jesus.[28]

Second, when used in a negative sense, "the Jews" in John's Gospel are clearly not the Jewish people as a whole. In the preponderance of cases the term refers to the Jewish authorities.[29] As Raymond Brown ob-

27. Much depends here on proper sequencing. Do the attempts to kill Jesus come after his dysphemisms, or do the dysphemisms come after the attempts to kill Jesus? Does Jesus provoke the conflict, or is the conflict thrust upon him without any moral — as distinct from religious — wrongdoing on his part?

28. What has happened in John to the injunction in the synoptic Gospels to love enemies and bless those who curse you (Luke 6:27-28)? A similar thing as has happened to this injunction in the synoptic Gospels themselves when Jesus, for a seemingly lesser offense than the one registered in John, denounces the Pharisees as "fools" and "unmarked graves" (Luke 11:37-53). There may be a difficulty in reconciling the stance of Jesus toward the Jews in John with the love of enemies demanded in the synoptic Gospels, but an analogous difficulty exists when one tries to reconcile the injunctions and behavior of Jesus *within* the Synoptics.

29. As the subsequent history of relations between Christians and Jews shows, the substitution that the Gospel writer undertakes — describing Jewish authorities as "the Jews" — is open to dangerous misunderstandings and, especially in the light of that history, ought to be avoided. It is easy to see, however, how John's substitution came about. During

serves, "John can refer interchangeably to 'the Jews' and to the chief priests and Pharisees (compare 18:3 and 12; 8:13 and 22), and . . . John speaks of 'the Jews' where [the] Synoptic Gospels speak of the Sanhedrin (compare John 18:28-31 with Mark 15:1)."[30] In *all* cases, "the Jews" refers to *concrete persons* who are in conflict with Jesus. There are no instances of negative comments about the Jews in John where it is not clear that ex-treme conflict is in view. On the other hand, there are many instances in which "the Jews" is used either in a neutral sense, as when Joseph and Nicodemus are said to be burying Jesus according to the custom of the Jews (19:40), or in a decidedly positive sense, as when it is said that salva-tion is of the Jews and Jesus identifies himself as a Jew (4:22).

Why was Jesus an object of the hatred of "the Jews," according to the Gospel? Because he healed a man on the Sabbath, a day when their reli-gious sensibilities said that no work should be done, and, above all, be-cause he had an inordinately high opinion of himself in that he was mak-ing himself equal with God, which according to those same religious sensibilities constituted blasphemy (5:18; 10:33). It is on his "teaching" that the trial before Jewish authorities after his arrest concentrated, not on any of his alleged misdeeds (18:19), not on any of his "wrongdoings." How did Jesus respond to repeated attempts to kill him? Not only did he not use violence, he withdrew on occasion from the regions of immedi-ate threat. Most significantly, the Gospel interprets Jesus' eventual death at the hands of Jewish authorities — and places this interpretation in the mouth of Jesus himself (8:27) — as his giving of his life *on their behalf as the ones who had wronged him!* For certainly they were included in the world that God loved (3:16), whose savior Jesus was (4:42), and whose sin

---

the 1990s war in the former Yugoslavia, we all used to talk about "the Serbs," for instance, as shelling Osijek, although it was not the Serbs but their military and political leaders who were undertaking the action and had done so without universal approval on the part of the Serbian population. In conversations, I would talk in the same way, even though I had pre-viously written about the dangers of both the dysphemic use of language and of the disre-gard of de facto differences within the sphere of the "other" (see Miroslav Volf, *Exclusion and Embrace: Theological Reflection about Identity, Otherness, and Reconciliation* [Nashville: Abingdon, 1996]). For me, the designation was shorthand, elicited in part by the fact that leaders, precisely because they are leaders, act on behalf of the whole even when those on whose behalf they act disagree with their actions. But it was a problematic shorthand.

30. Brown, *The Community of the Beloved Disciple*, 41.

he took away (1:29). Jesus' only form of opposition in the confrontation with the Jewish authorities was to pass evaluative judgments on them and their behavior. He called them the devil's children.

Were these judgments too harsh? What would *we* call people who would kill others for no other reason than that they help people on the wrong days and let others know of their excessively high opinion of themselves? What do *we* think of people who kill others for no other reason than that they have, from the perspective of these people, deviant religious views? We don't just call them intolerant; we call them evil, or at least we should. And if they pursue their murderous intentions on a massive scale, even the inhabitants of secularized European countries do not shy from using the term "demonic," as was the case during the wars in the former Yugoslavia or during the massacre in Rwanda. Eschew here all talk of good and evil, true and false, above and below, even godly and demonic, and seek instead to break down stark polarities whether in the name of liberal tolerance or poststructuralist "absolute hospitality," and you'll end up not only playing into the hands of murderers but in fact finding yourself an enemy of salutary social plurality.[31]

31. My point is not that the description of the Jews as the devil's children is justified on account of how they in fact treated Jesus. I am not pursuing that historical question here, and my point would stand even if it turned out that historically the Gospel is misrepresenting the way Jesus was treated by the Jewish authorities and the larger population. The only thing relevant to my project here is the character and function of oppositional dualities as we encounter them in the text of the Gospel.

One could argue, of course, that it was on account of his operating with oppositional dualities that John engaged in historical misrepresentations which, as such projections sometimes do, then justified applying oppositional dualities to the situation. However, the story of the relations between Jesus and the Jews must be more complicated than such projectionist accounts suggest. For if historical projection were at work, John would hardly have had a pervasively positive view of the Jews in the first four chapters (one possible exception being 2:18-20), and he would hardly have created an utterly negative view of the Jews — a group that obviously included the whole of John's community — only then to have them included among the objects of God's love for whom Jesus died. But even if John were inventing the Jews as persecutors, the invention would simply underscore that at the level of the text the employment of oppositional dualities in John presupposes the kind of violent situation that alone makes these dualities appropriate. John is saying that only those who do what the text says the Jewish authorities did ought to be called the "devil's children."

Neither is my point to deny that the statements about the Jews made by John have

Indeed the Jesus of John's Gospel reserved the negatives of his stark-est oppositional dualities for those who resisted with murderous vio-lence a pluralization of the cultural space by introducing into it an alter-native, overarching interpretation of life. The amazing thing is that, according to that same Gospel, Jesus gave his life for the salvation of those who murdered him and whose sins he was so uncompromisingly castigating. Therein, John does not differ markedly from what the rest of the New Testament says both about Jesus' death on the cross and about how Christians should treat their enemies. The narrative of John as a whole offers one large affirmation of what I take to be one of the extraor-dinary features of early Christianity: a combination of moral clarity that does not shy away from calling evildoers by their proper name, and of deep compassion toward them that issues in willing sacrifice of life itself on their behalf.

As the presence of this extraordinary feature of early Christianity in John makes plain, it is a major mistake to identify oppositional dualities in John and analyze them on their own, apart from how they are situated in the larger narrative of the Gospel. For then one will not have explored the concrete Johannine form and function of these dualities but only their abstract contours along with their possible uses and misuses. Once we situate John's oppositional dualities within his larger narrative — both the narrative account of the situation with which they are corre-lated and the larger pattern of action and thinking of the protagonist who employs them — the question will no longer be whether or not these dualities are salutary. The crucial and exceedingly difficult ques-

---

been used by Christians over the past two thousand years to justify egregious mistreat-ment of the Jewish people as a whole. Such real uses rest on an evil-intentioned selec-tive reading of the text, I believe. The reaction of Christians to their "mistreatment" by the Jews was not ethical condemnation of the mistreatment along with action on behalf of the Jews, as would be appropriate if the example of John's Jesus were followed; it was, on the contrary, persecution and murder of Jews. Moreover, Christians illegitimately read *past* mistreatment of Jesus by Jewish leaders as legitimizing present revenge by Christians against Jewish people who lived centuries later. To use the narrative of John to justify the persecution of Jews is to place it on its head: Persecuted Jews become the "Jesus" of the narrative, and persecuting Christians become "the Jews." The narrative is thereby made to legitimize precisely the kind of behavior it was originally intended to combat.

tion will be that of identifying properly in concrete situations what is legitimately to be described as "from below," "false," "evil," etc. The key question is not whether the Johannine kind of oppositional dualities should be used, but how to use them wisely.

Religious Pluralism

"Religious pluralism" is an ambiguous term. On the one hand, it can be used to denote the coexistence of many religions in a single social space, in which case it is a species of pluralism as a social fact. The contemporary world is not only culturally plural, it is also religiously plural; indeed, it is culturally plural partly because it is religiously plural. If we consider the world as a whole, it is unclear whether there is a decrease of religious plurality as a consequence of the general decrease in cultural plurality or an increase on account of the emergence of new religious movements inside and outside Christianity. But certainly in Western countries there is a growing awareness of religious pluralism, an awareness triggered both by the mass media's communicating information about other religions and by the spread of other religions within Western cultural spaces.[32]

On the other hand, "religious pluralism" can be also used to denote a way in which adherents of a religion should relate to other religions, as well as to their own. In this sense, religious pluralism is a species of pluralism as a philosophical stance, and it represents in part a response to the fact of religious plurality. Theological academic culture uses the term "religious pluralism" predominantly in this sense and designates by it the view that all major religions enjoy rough parity as ways to salvation. It is not that one is true and the others false; all are true, and all are true to more or less the same extent.

What is John's relation to religious pluralism as a normative stance? He will have none of it. Of course, John advocates neither the use of vio-

---

32. For an account of the pluralization of the United States see, for instance, Diana L. Eck, *A New Religious America: How a 'Christian Country' Has Become the World's Most Religiously Diverse Nation* (San Francisco: HarperCollins, 2001).

lence nor the employment of political or social pressure to reduce religious pluralism. Even if boundaries are vigilantly maintained, there are no traces of the will to impose by force the one true religion on others, only signs of resisting others' attempts forcibly to limit the Johannine community's free exercise of religion.[33] But it is also clear that, if we were to follow the famous and in many ways inadequate typology of possible stances toward other religions, John would properly be described neither as a pluralist nor as an inclusivist but as a particular kind of exclusivist. For John, as for many other exclusivists, that label is inadequate partly because it is applied solely on the basis of how a given religion is perceived to relate to other religions. A description better suited to John would be that the Gospel's stance is particularist. For the text is less interested in negating other religions as ways of salvation than affirming a particular person, Jesus Christ, as the universal savior. The claim "no one comes to the Father except through me" (14:6b) is a consequence of the claim that Jesus is "the way, and the truth, and the life" (14:6a), not the other way around. Substantively, of course, exclusivist and particularist positions amount to the same, except that in the first, the primary emphasis is on negation, whereas in the second, it is on affirmation.

Everything in John speaks against the view that regards all world religions as more or less equally true and roughly equally adequate ways of salvation. The pluralist position is ruled out. So is the inclusivist position. With the exception of Judaism, John does not seem to think of other religions as containing fragmentary truths that find fulfillment in Christ. We may be tempted to read in an inclusivist way the claim that the Word, which is the "true light," enlightens "everyone" (1:9). All people are enlightened by the light that comes from the Word, and all religions are true to the extent to which this light shines through them. Jesus, who is "the way, the truth, and the life" (14:6), would then be the concrete and unsurpassable incarnation of that one and universal light.[34] An inclusiv-

33. We should keep in mind that what we, the moderns, call religion is not quite the same phenomenon as what, for instance, early Christians were embracing when they became followers of Christ. Religion as a discrete sphere of life is very much a modern phenomenon. Yet it is hard to know what other general term to use for the self-identity of early Christians qua Christians.

34. The contemporary inclusivist position owes much to John's Gospel. It is on ac-

ist reading of John stumbles, however, on his oppositional dualities. Though the Word enlightens everyone, there are people who do not believe in Jesus, remain in darkness, and are therefore objects of God's wrath (3:36). They have effectively shut themselves off from the light (or, given John's theology of election, God has not drawn them to the light).

What are we to make of John's exclusivism? It is often assumed that all forms of exclusivism are problematic. But I am not persuaded that the pluralist and inclusivist alternatives are substantively less problematic. A pluralist approach to world religions — an approach that emphasizes rough parity between them — has to postulate something like the existence of an unknowable "Real" behind all religions,[35] or at least has to insert all religions into a broader framework of meaning.[36] In either case, pluralism not only fails to respect religions in their concreteness, in the first case by looking through them to their core and in the second case by making them an instance of something more encompassing. Significantly, pluralism also cannot fail to reinstate exclusivism; only the scope of what is in has expanded. Some religions are still more equal than others. In a pluralist view, Buddhists, for instance, espouse true religion, whereas Branch Davidians do not.[37]

An inclusivist approach to world religions — which emphasizes that all that is true in other religions comes from the God Christians worship

---

count of the incarnation of the Logos, argues Karl Rahner as the chief of inclusivists, that each human being is endowed with a "supernatural existential," so that the relation to the Word, whether it is recognized or not, belongs to the conditions of the possibility of humanity. So all people are in an important sense in, and various religions are more or less adequate ways of thematizing and living out this being in (see Karl Rahner, *Foundations of Christian Faith* [trans. William V. Dych; New York: Seabury, 1978]).

35. John Hick, *An Interpretation of Religion* (New Haven: Yale University Press, 1989).

36. See Michael Barnes, *Theology and the Dialogue of Religions* (Cambridge: Cambridge University Press, 2002).

37. Gavin D'Costa has plausibly and forcefully argued for this point in "The Impossibility of a Pluralism View of Religions," *Religious Studies* 32 (June 1996): 223-33. At the *religious* level, pluralism is exclusivistic, though its exclusivism is broader than that of classical exclusivism. A pluralist can affirm that a number of religions — in fact, all world religions but not some sects — are mutually nonexclusive and equally true, whereas a classical exclusivist affirms that all other religions but her own are false. Pluralism is also exclusive as a *theory of religion* — it excludes "most forms of orthodox belief, Christian or otherwise" (229).

— insinuates the Christian faith or the God of the Christian faith into other religions against the self-understanding and wishes of the adherents of these religions. There is something deeply troubling in a patronizing and colonizing sort of way about calling representatives of other religions "anonymous Christians." And of course, exclusivity is not banned from inclusivism; for everything that does not conform to the Christian normative revelation is excluded. Both pluralism and inclusivism, argues Gavin D'Costa correctly, are "sub-types of exclusivism."[38]

A Peculiar Kind of Exclusivism

Some form of exclusivism is the only game in town. Exclusivists rightly recognize and unapologetically affirm as much. Exclusivism also has the merit of respecting the self-understanding of other religions and engaging them seriously at the level of their truth claims. It may breed a sense of superiority, of course; but if it is not absolutist, it will allow at least the possibility of its own wrongness and its competitors' rightness. It may also lead to violent suppression of other religions, though not if accompanied with a commitment to nonviolence. It is unclear how to decide whether John's exclusivism is absolutist or not. There can be no doubt, however, of John's commitment to nonviolence (18:36).

To name John's attitude toward other religions "exclusivist" is to concentrate on the negative, on what it denies other religions. But crucial for a religion is not just how it views its competitors as ways of salvation but above all how it understands its own identity in relation to them. Identity can be defined oppositionally and exclusively: I am self-enclosed, and I am what the other is not. Identity can also be defined nonoppositionally and inclusively: I am from the start inhabited by the other, and I am partly what the other is.[39] Central to the oppositional and nonoppositional definition of identity is not so much the question of the presence of otherness in the self, for some otherness is always present in

38. D'Costa, "The Impossibility of a Pluralism," 225.
39. See Miroslav Volf, "Living with the Other," *Journal of Ecumenical Studies* 39/1-2 (2002): 8-25.

the self. Central is rather the *recognition* on the part of the self of the presence of otherness in the self.

How does John construe Christian identity in relation to other "religions"? The only way to answer this question is to look at John's relation to Judaism. As I argued earlier, we should read negative descriptions of the Jews as referring to those who were persecuting Jesus and not to the Jewish people or the Jewish religion. On the whole, John valorizes positively Jewish religious institutions. True, Jesus speaks of "your law" (8:17; 10:34; 7:19, 22) "as if he were a non-Jew."[40] But the distancing can be at least partly accounted for by the polemical situation of separated communities engaged in conflict without postulating that John believed that the Hebrew scripture, including the Law, was invalid for Christians; in fact, he appeals to the Law's and to Moses' testimony to Jesus. John's attitude toward the temple is similar. The prophecy about "true worshipers" who will "worship the Father in spirit and truth" notwithstanding (4:19-24), John interprets Jesus' cleansing of the temple not as a rejection of it but as "zeal for your [God's] house" and has Jesus describe it as "my Father's house" (2:16-17). Consider also the role of Caiaphas, the high priest, who "prophesied that Jesus was about to die for the nation" (11:51). He was not used by God irrespective of who he was, like Balaam's donkey; he prophesied, John says, by virtue of his office — which is to say that the office had to be valorized positively by John even though he himself is clearly out.[41] Most significantly, it is John, and John alone of all the New Testament writers, who states unambiguously that "salvation is from the Jews" (4:22) and in the process identifies himself with the Jews by claiming that "we — the Jews — worship what we know" (4:22). Recent scholarship has recognized the essential Jewishness of John.[42] The claim of

40. Bultmann, *Theology of the New Testament*, 2:5.

41. According to Augustine, the Evangelist attributes the fact that through a bad man a spirit of prophecy predicts things to come "to a Divine Sacrament, in that he was pontiff, i.e., high priest" (Augustine, *Homilies*, 2:667). In Augustine's view, John recognizes the office of the high priest to have sacramental power. Whether or not one understands the office in sacramental terms, it is clear that the fact of having the office of the high priest makes it appropriate that he should prophesy the sacrificial death of God's lamb.

42. Of course, John's being Jewish does not in and of itself mean that John is not, at the same time, anti-Jewish. But I have already addressed that question.

John's Jesus that "no one comes to the Father but by me" (14:6b) notwith-standing, John was aware of and affirmed the origins of the Christian faith in the Jewish religion, the continuing significance of the pillars of that religion for the Christian faith, and the Christian faith's persisting commonalities with the Jewish religion.

The remarkable thing is that this, on the whole, positive relation to Judaism was formulated not at a safe distance from the synagogue but as John's community was, from its own perspective, experiencing persecution by the Jewish authorities. John's oppositional dualities can accommodate the kind of communal identity that is not forged through negation of religious otherness but is comfortable with the presence of otherness within its own boundaries. As I will argue below, there are other strong indicators in the Gospel of this kind of understanding of community identity.

Sectarianism?

I have suggested that it is not enough to highlight the presence of oppositional dualities in John and that to understand their character and function, we need to pay attention to their concrete shape. One way to place under the magnifying glass Johannine oppositional dualities is by examining the thesis, often put forward in recent decades by friend and foe, that John is a sectarian. In what follows I will *not* argue that John is *not* a sectarian. It may well be that in modern terms "sect" describes the Johannine bunch better than any other category readily available. I have no stake in the debate on whether or not John is sectarian; the answer is hardly illuminating, given that the actual line between the ideal types of "church" (or denomination) and "sect" is drawn arbitrarily on a continuum extending, say, from a complete rejection of the world to its complete acceptance.[43] But I contend that if John is a sectarian, he is a sectarian of a rather surprising sort.

43. See Benton Johnson, "On Church and Sect," *American Sociological Review* 28 (1963): 542. Sometimes theologians and biblical scholars write about "sects" as though this designation were not an ideal type, significant as a heuristic device but not to be encountered in reality, "where different types mingle and combine with each other"

Most of those who do contend that John is a sectarian — who advocate what I will call the sectarian thesis — think that John is a very typical sectarian, indeed an almost ideal-typical sectarian. A good example is Robert H. Gundry, who in his book titled *Jesus the Word According to John the Sectarian* argued with clarity and power that John "sees only in black and white."[44] The claim does not bear close scrutiny, however. We see in fact shades of gray on both the white and black sides of the divide, which is to say that John's oppositional dualities are much more open to inner differentiation, and therefore to plurality, than advocates of the sectarian thesis allow. I will try to show this openness by exploring three interconnected but distinct issues about John's community: (1) its relation to outsiders, (2) the nature of its boundaries, and (3) the character of its identity.

Outsiders

Consider John's *relation to outsiders*. Many exegetes argue that John has an utterly negative view of the "world" — the things and the people of the world. Outside are darkness, falsehood, evil, and Satan's kingdom of

---

(Troeltsch, *The Social Teaching of the Christian Churches*, 995). A theologian, possibly unlike a sociologist, should not be content with assigning groups to ideal types but should explore the inner complexity of a given ecclesial community or, as is the case in my engagement with John, the central texts of a given community. Ideal types are abstractions; theologically more important are concrete realities. Moreover, in interpreting a community or its central texts, it is important not simply to attend to what it says in its overarching theological statements but to see these statements in conjunction with what we could call the community's microconvictions and micropractices — the many ways in which it goes about living and thinking in concrete situations that are simply not deducible from the overarching convictions, and indeed qualify such convictions in creative ways, thereby specifying how these convictions should be understood. In the following, I will try to attend to John's Gospel in its concreteness, rather than inquiring as to what ideal type the community that produced it ought to be assigned, and I will do so by examining a combination of overarching statements, microconvictions, and micropractices that come to light in the text.

44. Robert H. Gundry, *Jesus the Word According to John the Sectarian: A Paleo-fundamentalist Manifesto for Contemporary Evangelicalism, especially its Elites, in North America* (Grand Rapids: Eerdmans, 2002), 66.

death; inside are light, truth, goodness, and God's kingdom of life. Jesus is never said to love the world, and though in John believers are not outright commanded not to love the world, as they are in 1 John, they are not explicitly encouraged to do so either. The world is evil, and the proper attitude toward it, so it is suggested, is antipathy. There are some instances of sympathetic attitudes to the evil world, the advocates of this position admit. God loves the world (3:16), and Jesus gives himself for the life of the world (1:29; 6:51), for instance. But advocates of the sectarian thesis either relegate these instances to the community's history and read them as "another example of the fact that the community does not erase its past"[45] or deem them insignificant for the overall valuation of the world by believers.[46]

But neither of these ways of reading statements about sympathetic attitudes toward the world can be correct. To take up claims about God's love for the world and Jesus' bearing the sin of the world into the Gospel means not only not to erase the past but also to let the past shape the present. For the text never tags these references as a rejected past. On the contrary, they are crucial for the narrative of the Gospel as a whole. Drop references to God's love of the world and to the Son's coming into the world for the world's salvation, and the entire Gospel collapses because the main motor that pushes the action toward the cross and the resurrection has failed.[47]

---

45. Brown, *The Community of the Beloved Disciple*, 63, n. 111.

46. Gundry, *Jesus the Word*, 51-69.

47. Wayne Meeks does not contest the presence or even prominence in the Gospel of the affirmation that God loves the world. But he notes that such affirmation was "doubtless hard to keep in mind for a sect that perceived itself so hated by the world" (Wayne A. Meeks, "The Ethics of the Fourth Evangelist," in *Exploring the Gospel of John: In Honor of D. Moody Smith* [ed. R. Alan Culpepper and C. Clifton Black; Louisville: Westminster John Knox, 1996], 323). No doubt the more hostility one encounters, the more difficult it is to think of your God as loving your enemy. But if it was hard for the Johannine sect to keep in mind God's love for the world, presumably it would have been even harder for it to structure the whole Gospel around such an affirmation and enactment of divine self-giving love. Emphasis on God's love notwithstanding, one could claim, as Käsemann does, that in John there is no feeling of solidarity with the world (Käsemann, *The Testament of Jesus*, 66). But what if instead of "solidarity" one used "charity"? The claim would not stand, provided one took seriously not only God's self-

The second way of dealing with the instances of sympathetic attitudes toward the world — namely by claiming that God's loving relation
to the world would have no impact on a believer's valuation of the world
— seems utterly implausible. After all, believers are explicitly sent into
the world *"as"* the Son was sent by the Father (17:18; 20:21). Jesus embodied God's love for the world both in doing good — feeding the hungry
(6:5-16), healing the sick (4:46-54; 5:2-9; 9:1-7; 11:11-27), giving money to
the poor (13:29 by implication) — and ultimately in giving his life for the
salvation of the world. By being sent as Jesus was sent, believers are commanded to do the same.[48] For Jesus and for the believers to do all these

---

giving love but also Jesus' direction to give money to the poor and especially his miracles. Käsemann believes that meeting human need was "at most a subsidiary aim" of
miracles (Käsemann, *The Testament of Jesus,* 21). But that cannot be correct. With the
exception of thunder from heaven (12:29), John records exclusively miracles that help
people — and help outsiders more often than insiders. The use of the term "signs" for
miracles changes nothing in this regard; it does not reduce miracles to symbols of salvation but underscores one purpose of the miracles, namely, to elicit faith in Jesus. For it is
clear how *any* miraculous deed performed by Jesus could demonstrate his power, but it
is not clear how it could symbolize *salvation* without helping persons. It is noteworthy
also that the debates about the Sabbath center around Jesus' "doing good."

48. Wayne Meeks grants that John does present Jesus as the model for people to
follow but argues that Jesus is in fact not "imitable." He is "too alien to human weakness
to provide a convincing model, too much 'the god striding over the face of the earth'"
(Meeks, "The Ethics of the Fourth Evangelist," 318). It is a matter of debate whether and
to what extent — as Käsemann has most passionately argued in his *Testament of Jesus*
— John portrays Jesus as a god striding over the face of the earth. The kinds of
exegetical acrobatics Käsemann has to undertake in order to make this thesis stick
along with its ecclesiological implications should serve as a warning (see also Marianne
Meye Thompson, *The Humanity of Jesus in the Fourth Gospel* [Philadelphia: Fortress,
1988]). But even if the Gospel did portray Jesus in such a fashion, it is not clear that this
portrayal would preclude him from serving as an imitable model. Imitation of *divinity* is
a common religious theme. And throughout the centuries, Christians have never felt it
odd that they should be required to be "perfect . . . as [their] heavenly Father is perfect"
(Matthew 5:48) but have implicitly or explicitly adjusted their understanding of their
own possible perfection so as to take into account that they are human and their Father
divine. (For a philosophical discussion on the imitation of God as the foundation of ethics, see Linda Zagzebski, "The Virtues of God and the Foundation of Ethics," *Faith and
Philosophy* 15 [1998]: 538-53.) Moreover, in John, Jesus models self-giving love, which is
more or less the way the other New Testament writings present Jesus as a model (see
Luke T. Johnson, *The Real Jesus* [San Francisco: HarperSanFrancisco, 1996]).

things *is*, in the relevant sense, to *love* the world in all but name — a world hostile to them, as John repeatedly underscores.[49] Does the absence of the command to love the world (or, for that matter, the presence in 1 John of the command *not* to love the world) signal disapproval of believers' benevolence and beneficence toward unbelievers? I do not see how such an argument could be made on the basis of the Gospel.

But in John, Jesus does not even *pray* for the world, protest those who believe that thereby they have clinched the argument. "I am asking [praying] on their behalf [i.e., on behalf of those who have believed]; I am not asking on the behalf of the world, but on behalf of those whom you gave me, because they are yours" (17:9). According to some commentators, the verse implies that Jesus refuses to pray for the world in general, not just that he does not pray for it on this specific occasion.[50] I am not persuaded. As Rudolf Bultmann points out, Jesus in fact *does* end up praying for the world in the remainder of the prayer: ". . . so that the world may believe . . . so that the world may know . . ." (17:21, 23).[51] One explicit *goal* of his prayer for the disciples' preservation and unity is "the eventual salvation of the *world*."[52]

---

49. Along with many other interpreters, David Rensberger talks about "John's sectarian hostility toward outsiders" (David Rensberger, *Johannine Faith and Liberating Community* [Philadelphia: Westminster, 1988], 139). I see nothing of the sort in John. First, critique or even sharp critique is not the same as hostility but can be an expression of love. John combines Jesus' critique of those who hate Jesus with his dying on their behalf. Second, this critique, which is read as hostility, is not directed indiscriminately toward outsiders but toward very specific outsiders, those who are (from the perspective of the author of the text) seeking to harm Jesus and his disciples.

50. See, for instance, Rudolf Schnackenburg, *The Gospel According to John,* vol. 3 (trans. Kevin Smyth; London: Burns & Oates, 1968-82), 178; C. K. Barrett, *The Gospel According to St. John* (New York: Macmillan, 1957), 422.

51. Rudolf Bultmann, in his *The Gospel of John: A Commentary* (trans. G. R. Beasley-Murray; ed. R. W. N. Hoare et al.; Philadelphia: Westminster, 1971), writes, "God's love which is effective in the Son reaches out over the whole world (3.16); and in so far as the prayer for the community also means praying that the world may be won over through it (vv. 21, 23), to this extent the world is included in the intercession" (500).

52. Barnabas Lindars, *The Gospel of John* (Grand Rapids: Eerdmans, 1981), 566 (italics added). In his *Explanatory Notes Upon the New Testament* (London: Epworth, 1966), John Wesley puts the point as well as anybody else: "'I pray not for the world' — Not in these petitions, which are adapted to the state of believers only. (He prays for the world

Moreover, John's portrayal of the relation between the Father, the Son, and believers makes the simultaneous affirmation of God's love for the world and the denial of Jesus' and believers' love for the world virtually impossible. For the Father, who loves the world, does not just command while the Son and believers simply obey (10:18; 14:31). If the relation of the three were that of obedience only, the Father would love the world, and the Son and believers would out of obedience enact that love without sharing it. But in the Gospel, more important than obedience is the relation of mutual indwelling between the three agents, which logically precedes the relation of command and obedience. The Father dwells in the Son, and the Son dwells in believers (17:21), so that, all the differences between them notwithstanding, the Father's action can be described as the Son's action (14:10) and the Son's action as the believers' action. With the Son's agency construed as tied up with the Father's, and the believers' agency tied up with the Son's, we cannot plausibly read John as ascribing love of the world to the Father but denying it to the Son and believers.

We could take the absence of the command to love the world as a prohibition from associating with nonbelievers.[53] But that will not do either. Jesus and his disciples not only attended a wedding of nonbelievers, but Jesus also helped make it a more jovial occasion by turning water into wine (2:1-12). As his initial unwillingness to perform the miracle suggests, he had attended the wedding in response to an invitation (2:2), without originally intending to manifest his glory by performing the miracle (2:12). Whereas the synoptic Gospels consistently see Jesus' associating and even eating with publicans and sinners as part of his mission (Mark 2:15-17), in John his participation in a nonbelievers' feast seems originally divorced from that mission. At least initially, he participated not qua the savior of the world but qua friend or relative of unbelievers. That the miracle he eventually performed "revealed his glory" and that it may symbolize the transformation of Judaism (water) into the gospel

at 17:21.23, that they may believe — That they may know God hath sent him.) This no more proves that our Lord did not pray for the world, both before and afterward, than his praying for the apostles alone, 17:6-19, proves that he did not pray for them also which shall believe through their word, 17:20" (32).

53. Robert Gundry, in personal communication.

(wine) does not change the nature of his participation in the feast. Clearly, then, John does not prohibit association with nonbelievers. He implicitly encourages it.

Fostering the world's material and spiritual well-being and participating in its feasts are not what we would expect from those who see the world utterly negatively. We would also not expect them to eschew *condemning* the world. Instead we would expect them to hurl threats of divine wrath against it. But doing so is not what John's Jesus does. The theme of divine judgment *is* present. Jesus spoke of God's wrath against unbelievers (3:36) and understood himself as the executioner of that judgment in the end time (5:27-29). But he stated repeatedly and emphatically that he did *not* come into the world to judge it but to save it (3:17; 12:47). True, his coming into the world *effected* judgment, depending on how people responded to it (3:17-21). But that is precisely the point: *He* does not actively judge, *his words and actions* judge, depending on how people respond to them (3:17-21). John does have many negative things to say about the world, but startlingly he combines them with a noncondemnatory and utterly loving attitude toward the world rather than antipathy for it.

Boundaries

What is John's account of *the boundaries between believers and unbelievers?* Oppositional dualities raise expectations of razor-sharp boundaries. If John thinks only in stark polarities, the line separating the community from the rest will be thin, and there will be no gray zones on either side. But this picture is not what we find in the Gospel. On the negative side there is also a gray zone alongside the people ("the Jews") explicitly described by the text as children of the devil (8:44). In that zone are the adherents of John the Baptist. Though their teacher is likely in (3:25-36), they themselves seem to be out but are still not portrayed negatively. Furthermore, there are disciples of Jesus who do not believe, or have an incomplete faith (6:60-66). There are secret Christians who remain within the synagogue; they were not only disciples of Jesus but also believe in him, though they were afraid of being "put out of the synagogue"

(12:42-43). Neither should we forget disagreements about Jesus within the crowd: Those who think of him as a prophet or as the Messiah (7:40-43) are not seen as negatively as those who side with the Jewish authorities, see him as demon-possessed, and want to arrest and kill him (7:19, 40). Finally, to the gray zone belongs even Caiaphas, as I argued earlier.[54] The point of highlighting all these different kinds of reactions to Jesus is not simply to indicate the existence of plurality in the world but also to draw attention to the fact that John *evaluates* differences explicitly or implicitly in various — more or less positive — ways.[55] None of these people may have saving faith; therefore, in a significant sense they may be out, yet the Gospel differentiates among them and sees them not simply as in starkly negative but in partly positive terms.

Even more significant than the shades of gray on the negative side is the thick gray belt on the positive side. It is represented by what Raymond Brown has called "Apostolic Christians," symbolized by Peter and other members of the Twelve. They are outside the community of the Beloved Disciple but not outside the community of believers. Johannine Christians may have felt themselves superior to the Apostolic Christians but did not consider the Apostolic Christians as being outsiders, rather, insiders. Even if the existence of Apostolic Christians in John is not plausible, the fact of inner differentiation of those who are inside still remains. It seems that, with the possible exception of the Beloved Disciple,

54. Many interpreters of John read the harshest statements about the Jews as indicative of what John thinks about the outsiders as a whole (Bultmann, *Theology of the New Testament*, 2:16). But such a reading both fails to note that in John the Jews are a specific group, and not the whole people let alone the whole unbelieving world, and disregards the entire range of opinions expressed about outsiders in John. In such readings John appears almost anti-Jewish, but if anti-Jewishness is at work, it is that of the interpreters and not of John.

55. A test for this thesis is the question of the "world's" hatred of Jesus and of believers. The world loves its own but hates what is not of the world (15:18-19); that stance is characteristic of the world. Most of the groups in the gray zone listed above cannot be said to hate either Jesus or believers. Rather, they are not prepared to follow him, they are "scandalized" by Jesus' teaching, they are secretly his disciples, or they defend him publicly, which is to say they do not hate him. Of the groups mentioned above, only Caiaphas can be said to hate Jesus. He is, of course, a representative of a larger group that seeks to kill Jesus.

nobody really "gets it" despite the fact that all the disciples except Judas are clearly in (17:12). And as Stephen Motyer has argued, in the second part of the Gospel some of Jesus' disciples (Thomas, Philip, and Judas) are cast in the mold of Jesus' opponents from the first part.[56]

Then there is the figure of Nicodemus. It is not clear from the Gospel whether he is in or out, and that very lack of clarity is significant. He comes to Jesus at night, admits from the start that "Jesus is a teacher who has come from God" (3:2), discusses inquisitively with Jesus, and does not leave him in disagreement. The next thing we know, he is defending Jesus before the Pharisees to whom Nicodemus belonged (7:53), and then he brings "a mixture of myrrh and aloes, weighing about a hundred pounds" — an excessive amount being a sure sign of his devotion to Jesus — in order to help properly bury Jesus. Is he a secret disciple and therefore possibly out? John does not say so, though he does describe Joseph of Arimathea, whom Nicodemus helped to bury Jesus, as such a disciple. Is he a believer? John does not say that either.[57] He lets Nicodemus blur the boundaries — not a sign of a mind that thinks only in stark polarities.[58] Sure, John operates with an "elect/non-elect" dualism, and so there is *ultimately* a firm line separating one from the other. But only God knows where that line is. The author of the Gospel seems comfortable with leaving things undecided, at least in some cases.

---

56. Stephen Motyer, "The Gospel of John and Judaism" (paper presented at the conference on "St. John and Theology" at the University of St. Andrews), 12.

57. Commentators generally read the three appearances of Nicodemus in John as a gradual progression in the direction of full, public faith (i.e., insider status) but recognize ambiguity in his status (see Lindars [*The Gospel of John,* 304], who speaks of him as "virtually a full believer"). This position is consistent with the tradition of reading Nicodemus as catechumen (see Augustine, *Homilies,* 1:167). Minority opinion is that Nicodemus remains outside (Wayne A. Meeks, "The Man from Heaven in Johannine Sectarianism," *Journal of Biblical Literature* 91 [1972]: 53-57; Rensberger, *Johannine Faith,* 37-41).

58. In general, what I have suggested about the plurality that exists inside the community and the blurring of boundaries fits well with the fact that in John, as Rudolf Schnackenburg has noted, "faith can exist more or less fully" (Schnackenburg, *The Gospel According to John,* 1:571).

Identity

What lends the most insight into the character of John's oppositional dualities is *what he meant by the inside,* for it is only against the backdrop of the inside that John evaluates the outside in negative terms. So to comprehend the nature of oppositional dualities, we must carefully study the nature of their *positive* poles. In them, we find a sketch of the alternative world that John opposes to "this world."

Two things are conspicuously missing in a community that operates with oppositional dualities and that we expect therefore to be sectarian in character: emphasis on moral law and emphasis on church organization, whether that organization is hierarchical or democratic in character. The reason why sects need law and organization is simple: Without behavioral rules and authoritative ways of enforcing them, it is difficult to maintain rigid boundaries and oppositional stances. In John, the whole burden of maintaining boundaries and securing internal cohesion falls on faith (understood as an affirmation of certain beliefs about Jesus and as personal allegiance to him) and love, both for God and for one another. In the absence of rules to specify what love is and with only the model of Jesus to follow (13:14; 15:9-17), and in the absence of rulers to enforce orthodoxy and with the whole community endowed with the Spirit to lead its members "into all the truth" (16:13), the life of the community will necessarily be characterized by a high degree of fluidity. The result will be permanent instability and great flexibility but certainly not sectarian rigidity. It could be that the sharp doctrinal divisions in 1 John were the result of the lack of rules and procedures to enforce them (1 John 2:18-27; 4:1-3). But if John's community as reflected in the Gospel had difficulties maintaining boundaries, the Gospel could be more legitimately accused of not being sectarian enough than of being too sectarian.

Closely related to the emphasis on love and the absence of law is John's understanding of identity, or rather a practice of identity, for nowhere in the Gospel is the question thematized as such. Recall the earlier distinction between oppositional/exclusive and nonoppositional/inclusive identities. The contrast between the realm of light and the realm of darkness will look rather different depending on which of these notions of identity is operative inside the community. John, I propose, operates with a nonoppositional and inclusive account of personal and communal identity. Even more, according to him this kind of identity lies at the heart of being itself, since it characterizes not only humans but also the creator of everything.

The Father is in the Son and the Son is in the Father, claims John repeatedly. The Father is not simply the other of the Son, and the Son is not simply the other of the Father. The difference from the Son notwithstanding, the Father is the Father precisely as the one who indwells the Son and is indwelt by the Son. The difference from the Father notwithstanding, the Son is the Son precisely as the one who indwells the Father and is indwelt by the Father.[59] Analogously, the Son is in believers, and they are in him (17:21-23). As the one sent by the Father, the Son's identity is open to include the believers; as those given to the Son by the Father and who have embraced the Son, believers are what they are on account of the Son's indwelling them. Finally, an analogous relationship holds true between believers, for their unity is patterned on the unity of the Father and the Son (17:20-21). On all three levels — intradivine, divine-human, and intrahuman — identity does not entail simple binary opposition. Given that more than one actor is involved in shaping the identity of each actor, the identities of none will be completely fixed and stable in advance but will change as persons interact.[60]

In the Gospel, the unity between persons at each of these levels and

59. For such an understanding of identity see Volf, *Exclusion and Embrace*, 128, 176-81.

60. John's affinity to such a complex notion of identity is reflected also in the literary practices of the Gospel. George MacRae has pointed to the bewildering variety of outside sources John is able to draw on to express the identity of Jesus (see George MacRae, "The Fourth Gospel and *Religionsgeschichte*," *Catholic Biblical Quarterly* 32 [1970]: 13-24). Harold Attridge has gone even further to analyze the disruption of stable identities in the Gospel as the Word enters the "flesh" of the written word: "If something quite spectacular happens to flesh when the Word hits it, something equally wondrous happens to ordinary words when they try to convey the Word itself" (Harold Attridge, "Genre Bending in the Fourth Gospel," *Journal of Biblical Literature* 121/1 [2002]: 21). That wondrous thing that happens to words is, according to Attridge, genre bending — the Gospel's attempt "to force its audience away from words to an encounter with the Word himself" (21).

among the levels rests ontologically on their mutual indwelling and is therefore intimately tied to such an account of identity. In addition, the unity is secured by self-giving love. The Son loves Father and therefore gives himself for the world; the Father loves the Son and therefore places all things into his hands (17:24); the Son loves believers and therefore gives himself for them (10:11; 15:13); believers love the Son (21:15) and therefore abide in him and emulate his example (15:1-17). Believers love each other as the Son loves them (13:34; 15:12).[61]

A practice of identity in which the binary opposites of internal communal identities — Father versus Son, Son (and Father) versus believers, one believer versus another — have been overcome, combined with emphasis on self-giving love rather than the rule of law, is an important dimension of the positive pole of the larger oppositional duality between the kingdom of truth, light, and life whose ruler is God, and the kingdom of falsehood, darkness, and death whose ruler is Satan. It is in part against the backdrop of the affirmation of this personal and communal identity that John passes negative judgments about the world. If it is also correct, as I have argued, that Johannine oppositional dualities do not negate pluralism either as a political project or as a social fact, then I am not sure what may stand in the way of calling these dualities salutary. Indeed, we may begin to see how salvation may depend not only on affirming the positive pole of these dualities but also on negating the negative.

---

61. Käsemann is correct in suggesting that the interpretation of "love" is "one of the cruxes of Johannine interpretation," but he is wrong in understanding love as "speaking the Word on the one hand and . . . receiving and preserving it on the other" (Käsemann, *The Testament of Jesus,* 61). He appeals mainly to 15:15 (where "love" does not appear) and to 17:24, where "the address" is *not* said to constitute the love between the Father and the Son. At the same time, he dismisses passages that directly describe the content of the love — selfless service and surrender to the point of death (15:13; 13:1) — as "not the characteristic Johannine manner of speaking of love" (61). So what is *not* stated in the Gospel is characteristic of John but what is repeatedly stated is not! Käsemann's interpretation of love is a central piece of his attempt to show John's "unreflected doceticism" (66), characterized primarily by disinterest in the transformation of earthly realities (70). But since his interpretation of love — a crux of Johannine interpretation — is so manifestly false, it casts a dark shadow over his overall interpretation of John.

Peculiar Politics

Whatever else John's Gospel is — and it is a complex text that can be read from many angles — it is certainly also a *political* document. Though it does not contain a justification of and program for the exercise of political authority, it does seek to regulate relations of power between people and communities. John is therefore broadly political. Oppositional dualities are an essential part of John's politics, and it is mainly against the political effects of these dualities that critics of John raise their voices. John is radically exclusivist in his hostility toward the whole world, they say, and insufferably arrogant about the virtues of his own community. In concluding my own explication of John's dualism, I will pull together some strands from the discussion above briefly to examine John's politics by engaging in a bit of imagining. To test my case, I shall use the extreme form of tension between inside and outside found in John.

Imagine you belong to a community — a world power such as the United States, or a nation such as Croatia that has recently declared its independence, or a strong state such as Israel, whose existence is precarious in a hostile environment. You have just been attacked by another country, and the attack included a successful attempt to kill your leader. This incident was not an isolated one, and you have reason to think that hostilities will continue. How do you respond? Imagine the following response.

You develop a theory that the unjust death of your leader at the hands of your enemies not only benefited your community (he was killed instead of many of you) but that, in some mysterious way, he was killed also on your enemies' behalf — indeed, that your leader has himself given his life on their behalf. You are religious, and though you know and state that God will judge the killers for their wrongdoing at the end of the age, you do not hurl at them threats of future punishment, let alone seek to participate in the execution of that punishment. Instead, you try to win them over to become your friends. You condemn what your enemies have done, but you do not fight them by physical force or social pressure. You only name their deed as evil and the instigators and perpetrators themselves as demonic. But each and every one of your won-over enemies who shows allegiance to your now-dead leader and the ideals for which he stood, you accept immediately as part of your community and consider them your brothers or sisters. You do not reject them on account of their past, whether that past included executing the most egregious violence against you or simply belonging to the enemy camp. Instead of deploying violence against them or finding other effective ways to curtail their power, you decide to shower them with beneficence: You feed their hungry, heal their sick, and give money to their poor. Even as you are exposed to the pressures of enmity, you do not form a tightly knit organization with strict rules to enforce conformity and guarantee security but insist that your way is the way of love for one another, the kind of love that makes you willing to give your lives for each other. You do all of this if you are out of your mind, if you are from a different planet, or — if John's politics comprise your model.

Compared with what states engaged in conflict in fact do — not just authoritarian states or dictatorships but also solid democratic states that do not wish to divorce politics from morality — the scenario sketched above seems utopian. For we normally fight our enemies, we punish with utmost severity attempts to kill our leaders, and we never let our leaders die without fighting for them. It is hard for us to bring ourselves to think, let alone publicly declare, that God loves our sworn and proven enemies; we want to wreak revenge on them rather than befriend them. We guard our boundaries; and if we ever admit our former enemies into our community, it is only after extensive testing of their loyalty. The more attacked we are, the more we enforce the internal cohesion of our group; and we certainly do not seek to solve our enemies' problems.

Someone may suggest that the comparison, though true in its description of each group, is false. For I am comparing apples and oranges — a religious community on the one side, and a state on the other. The comparison stands, however. The main significant difference concerns the extent of power at either's disposal and monopoly on the use of force; the state has significantly more power to wield and has a monopoly on the use of force, whereas a religious community, especially one with minority status, is powerless. If anything, a powerless religious community would be more prone to relate to its opponents in dualistic ways than would a powerful state. It would not be difficult to show that many religious and nonreligious communities (including academic communities!) within a state act in a situation of conflict in ways that are very analogous to — often worse than! — the way the state acts. And compared with how various communities act toward their enemies and how they construe their identities in the context of conflicts, John, I propose, looks positively saintly.[62] *Saint* John, after all.

62. One final comment is a qualification. My analysis of John's Gospel moved at the level of the text. The only history I presupposed was that visible in the text itself. One could object that at the level of actual history, John's community may well have been the guilty party, in which case the Gospel would be an attempt at either disingenuous or delusional self-justification, a work of an evildoer covering his tracks. To show that this is not likely, I would have to write a different paper. So the results of my essay have to be qualified: I claim that my argument is valid at the level of the text as we have it.

PART III

Of God and Mammon

CHAPTER FIVE

God Is Love: Biblical Reflections on a Fundamental Christian Claim in Conversation with Islam

───── ⌘ ─────

For Christians, the statement "God is love" comes as close as any three words can to giving a "definition" of God. The phrase is short, but the "object" it describes is immense — infinite as well as related to every finite thing and to all finite things together. How does one write on such an enormous topic in the space of a few short pages? The challenge is increased given that I am writing in the context of dialogue between Muslims and Christians about the *Common Word,* which is to say in a tension-filled intellectual space of wrestling to understand and articulate similarities of as well as differences between these two faiths with regard to what it means to love God and neighbor. To avoid overloading these pages with dense elaborations, I will limit myself to only a few brief and inescapably inadequate remarks.

What do Christians mean when they say that God is love? To answer this question briefly it is best, I believe, to go back to the scriptural text in which that phrase originally occurs: 1 John 4:7-12.

> Beloved, let us love one another, because love is from God; everyone who loves is born of God and knows God. Whoever does not love does not know God, for God is love. God's love was revealed among us in this way: God sent his only Son into the world so that we might live through him. In this is love, not that we loved God

but that he loved us and sent his Son to be the atoning sacrifice for our sins. Beloved, since God loved us so much, we also ought to love one another. No one has ever seen God; if we love one another, God lives in us, and his love is perfected in us.

Differences and Stumbling Blocks

Properly understood, this text sums up the whole of the Christian faith. As it turns out, it also names a number of Christian convictions on which there are major differences between Christians and Muslims. Some may suggest that it is unwise to discuss in an interfaith setting a text which mentions these controversial Christian convictions in such a blunt way. But failing to discuss them will not make them disappear from Scripture or from the hearts of its Christian readers. Sweeping the distinctiveness of our respective faiths under the rug is mostly a form of (unintentional) falsehood and (well-meaning) dissimulation. Nothing good can come of it. Instead, motivated by care for those of other faiths as well as for the common good, we should bring those differences (as well as similarities) into the open, work to understand them accurately, present them without unnecessary stumbling blocks, and learn from each other.

Admittedly, the very designation of Jesus Christ as "the Son" and the description of God as sending "his only Son" is a major stumbling block to Muslims. The Qur'ān considers anyone who calls Jesus the "offspring of God" to resemble *kāfirs* (infidels) from the past (*Surat al-Tawba* 9:30). Most Muslims hear in the phrase "Son of God" a blasphemous claim that Jesus Christ was the offspring of a carnal union between God and a woman and that he is therefore an "associate" of God.

From the Christian point of view, this is a major misunderstanding — but unfortunately one whose force many Muslims feel at a psychologically very deep level. Christians unambiguously and emphatically reject any notion that Jesus Christ, let alone the eternal Son, is the offspring of a carnal union between God and an object of God's creation, and they reject equally the notion that the eternal Son is God's "associate." In the Scriptures, "the Son" (as in "the Son of God") is a *metaphor* for the particular closeness of Jesus Christ, the incarnate Word, to God and his special status as revealer of God (see Matt. 11:25-27; John 14:9). In later tradition, "the Son" (as in "God, the Son") is again a *metaphor* expressing the conviction that the Word, which was with God from eternity (John 1:1), is not some lesser divinity associated with God but is of the same "substance" with God and therefore belongs to the very being of the one and unique God. The irony of this particular stumbling block is that Christians not only do not mean by "Son of God" what most Muslims fear they do mean, but that Christians actually use the phrase to deny what most Muslims fear it expresses!

The comments on 1 John 4:7-12 that follow will be robustly theological rather than strictly exegetical; they are informed by an overarching reading of Scripture as a whole, as well as by a set of Christian convictions developed by great Christian teachers on the basis of such an overarching reading of Scripture. They are less in line with approaches of modern exegetes operating with a historical-critical method than they are with the style of interpreting that ancient commentators and church leaders such as St. Augustine (354-410) or Martin Luther (1483-1546) practiced.

Divine Being

The pivot of our text and the pivot of the whole of the Christian faith is the simple claim that God is love,[1] or, as Gregory of Nazianzus puts it more poetically, that God's "name is love."[2] Both the author of 1 John and his readers embrace this claim with such powerful conviction that he can introduce it in a mere subordinate clause (though he will repeat it again in a main clause only a few sentences later [v. 16]). To say "God is love" is not a static way of saying "God loves." Clearly, the author affirmed that God loves; he states so explicitly twice in our text (vv. 10, 11) and forty-six times in the whole epistle! Indeed, a major thrust of our text is

1. For a recent (2005) account of the whole of the Christian faith through the lens of the statement that "God is love," see the first encyclical letter of Pope Benedict XVI, *Deus Caritas Est* (http://www.vatican.va/holy_father/benedict_xvi/encyclicals/documents/hf_ben-xvi_enc_20051225_deus-caritas-est_en.html).

2. St. Gregory of Nazianzus, *Select Orations,* trans. Martha Vinson (Washington, D.C.: The Catholic University of America Press, 2003), 40.

that God loves — actively (God is engaged with humanity so that "we may live" [v. 9]) and abundantly (out of love God sends "his only Son" [v. 9], which is to say God's own very self).

The claim that God *is* love says more, however, than only that God loves. It names the character of God's being, not merely the nature of God's activity. It describes the divine Fountain from which the river of divine love flows. God's very being is love — so much so that the great church father St. Augustine could, maybe a bit too daringly, invert the claim and write: "Love is God."[3] Not just any kind of love, of course, and not love as mere interhuman activity, as though Augustine had anticipated Ludwig Feuerbach, the great nineteenth-century critic of religion whose method consisted in transmuting all claims about God into claims about humanity.[4] But love properly understood *is* God and God *is* properly understood love.

The relationship between God's being and God's activity is a complicated matter — in one important sense "God is" and "God loves" are identical[5] — and does not need to occupy us here. It will suffice to note one momentous consequence of the claim that God's active loving of humanity is rooted in God's being as love. Since the eternal God *is* love, God loves irrespective of the existence or nonexistence of creation; as the Gospel of John puts it, the "Father" loved the "Son" before the world began (John 17:24). If God's love were in any way tied to the creation, then the creation would be necessary for God to be love. But creation is not necessary for God and God does not become love with creation's coming into being. Instead, the contingent world is created by a God who already is love and just because God is love.

3. See Augustine, *Homilies on the Gospel according to St. John, and His First Epistle,* vol. 29 (Oxford: J. H. Parker, 1848), 7.4-5, p. 1182. Karl Barth, probably the greatest twentieth-century theologian, issues a warning: "If we say with 1 John 4 that God is love, the obverse that love is God is forbidden until it is mediated and clarified from God's being and therefore from God's act what the love is which can and must be legitimately identified with God" (Karl Barth, *Church Dogmatics,* II/1 [trans. T. H. L. Parker et al.; Edinburgh: T. & T. Clark, 1957], 276).

4. Ludwig Feuerbach, *The Essence of Christianity* (trans. George Eliot; New York: Harper Torchbooks, 1957).

5. So Karl Barth (*Church Dogmatics,* II/1, 283) from the perspective of understanding God's being as act (257-72).

Commenting on 1 John 4:9 the Protestant reformer John Calvin (1509-1564) writes:

> For if it be asked, why the world has been created, why we have been placed in it to possess the dominion of the earth, why we are preserved in life to enjoy innumerable blessings, why we are endued with light and understanding, no other reason can be adduced, except the gratuitous love of God.[6]

Similarly, the great Christian mystic Julian of Norwich (1342-1416) grounds creation in God's love:

> And in this love he has done all his works, and in this love he has made all things profitable to us, and in this love our life is everlasting. In our creation we had beginning, but the love in which he created us was in him from without beginning. In this love we have our beginning, and all this shall we see in God without end.[7]

The whole creation — everything that is not God — comes into existence on account of and within an already existing field of God's love, which defines the very being of God. As a character of God's being, God's love is as eternal as God is.

So God is love, and consequently God loves creatures; God is love, and consequently God's love is prior to there being any creatures. But who is it that God loves prior to creation? The object of God's pre-creation love cannot be different from God's own very self. But is God's love — God's self-love — then still properly to be called *love?*

Divine Differentiation

Many Christian theologians through the centuries have seen a close connection between the claim that God *is* love and the claim that God is the

6. John Calvin, Commentary on 1 John 4.

7. Julian of Norwich, *Showings* (trans. Edmund Colledge and James Walsh; New York: Paulist, 1978), 342-43.

Holy Trinity. Love implies, indeed requires, an object; "to love" is a transitive verb. If love is an essential attribute of God independent of the existence of everything that is not God, how could God be love if God were not, precisely as One God, somehow also differentiated in God's own being? Our text brings up the topic of divine differentiation implicitly in that it names two actors in the drama of God's love for the world: God and God's Son (for Christians *not* an "offspring" or an "associate," as I have said earlier and as will be clear also from what I say below). Our text itself is pre-Trinitarian, but to make proper sense of it we need to presuppose that God is the Holy Trinity — in relation to the world as well as in God's own being apart from the world.

Before exploring the relation between love and the triunity of the One God, it is important, especially in the context of a dialogue between Muslims and Christians, to state plainly what Christian theologians do not mean when they say that God is triune. First, God is *uncompromisingly one*. For Christians to affirm God's triunity is *not* to deny God's unity. In the first Christian centuries, all the intense and intricate debates about the Trinity were carried on precisely because the church fathers refused to compromise on the unity of God. Jesus, after all, affirmed the signature confession of his own Jewish people: "The Lord our God, the Lord is one" (Mark 12:29). God is either one, or there is no God. By definition, anything of which there can be two, or three, or more cannot be God in the proper sense of that term. Because the oneness of God was so important in the tradition of the great Christian thinkers, they insisted that the three divine "hypostases" subsist in a single, numerically identical divine substance.

Second, God is *utterly unique*. God alone is God. All else that exists is non-God. Moreover, there is a categorical, not merely a quantitative or even qualitative, difference between God and the world. God is not a member in a common household of being with other entities in the world. God is utterly unique. The text we are considering expresses this thought with a simple claim: "No one has ever seen God" (1 John 4:12). The reason why no one has seen God isn't that people have not looked hard enough or that they could not get to a place from which it would be possible to spot God; rather, God is such that God cannot be seen with physical eyes at all. As St. Augustine says, "not with the eye but with the heart must He be sought";[8] and the condition of seeing God with the eye of the heart is a transformation of the whole person to be "like God" (1 John 3:2).

Third, God is *beyond number.*[9] This affirmation follows from God's categorical uniqueness. It is impossible to count God as one among many other things that can be counted — all different things in the world plus one more object, maybe the biggest of them all and containing them all, called God. So when we say that there is only one God, we do not mean it in the same sense as when we say that there is only one sun or even only one universe. Similarly, great theologians of the past believed that it is impossible, strictly speaking, to count *in* God — naming one after another, as discrete "objects," all the different "things" that are in God. So when we say that there are "three" hypostases in God, we do not mean it in the same way as when we say that Jesus took three disciples with him to the mount of Transfiguration. All human language about God, including language about God's oneness and triunity, is inadequate. Both the talk of "one" and of "three" is analogous when applied to God.

If the One God is utterly unique and beyond number, why do Christians then speak of divine triunity? Christians believe that the Word was made flesh in Jesus Christ (see John 1:1-18; 1 John 4:2-3). From this belief, it follows that the one, utterly unique God, who is beyond all counting, is internally differentiated as the Speaker, the Word, and the Breath (as we might express the divine triunity on the basis of John 1:1, which reads: "In the beginning was the Word, and the Word was with God, and the Word was God"). In speaking about God's sending God's Son, our text employs names more usual in the New Testament and in the tradition: "Father" and "Son," to which "Holy Spirit" is added on the basis of other texts and weighty dogmatic considerations. The designations may differ, but what they designate remains the same: they name the internal differentiation of the One God, who is beyond number and categorically different from everything else, which is not God.

How is the internal differentiation of the One God related to the

8. Augustine, *Homilies* 7.10, p. 1186.

9. See Denys Turner, "The 'Same' God: Is There an Apophatic Solution, or, Who's to Know?" (paper presented at God and Human Flourishing Consultation, Yale Center for Faith and Culture, New Haven, CT, 2009).

claim that God is love? If God's being were *not* internally differentiated, how would we be able to say that (1) God *is* love in God's own eternal being, and that (2) God loves apart from God's relation to the world (because the world is contingent rather than necessary)? We could not. Without internal differentiation, God would love simply God's own self and be more properly described as Self-Love than as Love. As an incomparable and unique unity, however, God is an internally differentiated unity: there is "other" in the One God. And because there is "other" in God, there can be genuine love — love that does not merely affirm and celebrate the self, but love that gives to the other and receives from the other.[10] "You see a Trinity if you see charity," wrote St. Augustine in his justly famous book on the Holy Trinity.[11]

The First Love

Because God is the Holy Trinity, God's eternal love can be self-giving love rather than self-centered love. Consequently, God's love for humanity is a freely given love rather than a love motivated by the benefits that the object of love holds for the one who loves it. The one true God does not need anything from humans, but exists as self-complete and yet not self-enclosed plenitude of self-giving and other-receiving love. This circulating love, which is identical with the being of the One God, is the source of the world — the creaturely and therefore radically different other of God — and all its benefits.

If the eternal God *is* love in God's own self and in relation to creation, an important consequence follows: God's love is not a reactive love. And that takes us straight back to our text. "In this is love, not that we loved God but that he loved us" (1 John 4:10). A few verses later St. John writes that God's love is always "first" (v. 19), never second. St. Paul makes a similar point at the pinnacle of his epistle to the Romans: God never gives

10. There are significant Christian theologians who do not think that it is proper to speak of mutual love between the persons of the Trinity. A recent prominent exponent of this view is Karl Rahner (*The Trinity* [trans. Joseph Donceel; New York: Crossroad, 1998], 106).

11. Augustine, *The Trinity* (trans. Edmund Hill; Brooklyn: New City, 1991), 8, 12.

"in return" (Rom. 11:35). So God's love is always the first love; it is never simply a response to the character or behavior of things that are "outside" God. It cannot be otherwise if love is the very being of the eternal God.

In his *Heidelberg Disputation* the great Protestant reformer Martin Luther famously and a bit too sharply contrasted God's love for creatures and human love: "The love of God does not find, but creates, that which is pleasing to it. The love of man comes into being through that which is pleasing to it."[12] For humans, mostly, an encounter with what is pleasing *elicits* love; we experience something lovable — eating a gourmet meal, viewing a beautiful work of art, holding a newborn baby — and love is born in us. With God it is different, Luther claimed. Objects do not elicit God's love by their qualities; God's love creates objects together with their qualities. And if God does not find what is pleasing in an object — if human beings have become ungodly — God does not abandon the object in disgust until it changes its character. Instead, God seeks to recreate it to become lovable again.

God loved us "first" — before we loved God. This theme is common in the Old Testament. God's love is not elicited by any special virtues of the people of Israel (Deut. 7:7-8). Even more radically, according to the prophet Hosea, God's love remains first notwithstanding Israel's vices (11:1-11). The New Testament picks up and highlights the strand in the Old Testament that speaks of God's love notwithstanding human abandonment of God. In Romans, St. Paul writes of God's love for the "weak," the "ungodly," the "sinners," the "enemies" (5:6-10). Similarly, St. John underscores that out of love God sent Jesus Christ into the world not just "that we might live through him" (1 John 4:9) but, most pointedly, to be "the atoning sacrifice for our sins" (v. 10) and the sin of the whole world (2:2). God's love is "first" even toward sinners, the ungodly, the wrongdoers, and is not a response to anything they do — to their movement toward God or their emergent love of God.[13]

12. See Martin Luther, *Luther's Works* (St. Louis, Mo.: Concordia, 1957), 31:57.

13. Some scholars argue that in 1 John the world is not the object of God's love (as in St. John's Gospel [3:16]) but only its showplace (Luise Schottroff, *Der Glaube und die Feintliche Welt* [Neukirchen-Vlyn: Neukirchener Verlag, 1970], 287). But this argument does not take sufficiently into account the consequences of the fact that even if in

Infinite Love

For the most part, Muslims and Christians disagree about whether or not Christ died on the cross,[14] and if he did, whether he died as the atoning sacrifice for the sin of humanity. Here is not the place to discuss this important issue. As our interest is in the meaning of the phrase "God is love," I shall explore what Christ's atoning sacrifice implies about the character of God's love.[15]

First, God's love is *immeasurable.* "We know love by this, that he laid down his life for us" (3:16). Similarly, in St. John's Gospel Jesus, addressing his disciples, says: "No one has greater love than this, to lay down one's life for one's friends" (John 15:13). The greatest human love is a window into the infinity of divine love.

Second, God's love is *utterly gratuitous* and therefore *completely unconditional.* God does not love only those who are worthy of God's love, but loves all people, without any distinction.[16] As Jesus Christ said ac-

---

1 John God's loves extends only to the community of faith, God still loves them *notwithstanding* their sin. This "notwithstanding-character" of God's love effectively makes particularism pointless. Moreover, as Raymond Brown pointed out, "That the world has to be more than a showplace we see from 4:14 where 1 John speaks of Jesus as the 'Savior of the world'" (Raymond Brown, *The Epistles of John* [Garden City, N.Y.: Doubleday, 1982], 518).

14. But see Joseph Cumming, "Did Jesus Die on the Cross?" (paper presented at the Yale Center for Faith and Culture's Reconciliation Program, New Haven, CT, 2001).

15. It is crucial both to connect and to distinguish (1) God's eternal love apart from God's relation to the world and (2) God's love as manifest in overcoming the sin of the world. If we disconnect them, we lose the unity of the divine being. If we equate them, we project conditions of finitude and sin into the being of God. There is only one love of God that takes on a certain character in encounter with human sin. Thus we can speak of two forms of the one divine love. The first form of God's love — love of the eternal God apart from the world — is self-giving and mutually glorifying love. The second form of God's love — love of that same eternal God toward creatures — is in part a self-sacrificing love, and it is the response of the God of love to human sin and enmity toward God. The first form of love is basic, and it leads to the second form of love under the conditions of human sin. Not to differentiate adequately between the two forms of the one divine love is one of the most fundamental problems in the work of the great Catholic theologian Hans Urs von Balthasar (see on this Linn Tonstad, "Trinity, Hierarchy, and Difference: Mapping the Christian Imaginary" [Ph.D. diss., Yale University, 2009], 65-135).

16. On God's love as unconditional and indiscriminate see Miroslav Volf, *Free of*

cording to St. Matthew's Gospel, God "makes his sun rise on [both] the evil and on the good" (Matt. 5:45).

Third, God's love is *universal.* The One God is the God of all humanity; therefore the love that God is, is the love for all humanity, irrespective of any differences or divisions that exist between human beings. Absolutely no one is excluded and no deed is imaginable that would exclude anyone from God's love (though irredeemable wrongdoers — if there prove to be such people — will be excluded from "heaven" as God's world of love,[17] and be excluded not despite but because God's love is universal).

Fourth, God's love is *indiscriminately forgiving* of every person and for every deed. God is not just generous even to the unrighteous; God also forgives their unrighteousness so as to lead them through repentance back to the good they have abandoned. "If we confess our sins, he who is faithful and just will forgive us our sins and cleanse us from all unrighteousness" (1 John 1:9).

Finally, the *goal* of God's love is — *love.* The term 1 John uses to express this goal is "communion" (1:3) — communion of human beings with God, indeed, mutual indwelling of God and human beings (4:13-15), and communion of human beings with one another (1:7).

Love and Judgment

That God's love is immeasurable, unconditional, universal, and forgiving is but the consequence of the simple fact that God *is* love. Is then the all-loving God indifferent to human sin, condoning of ungodliness and wrongdoing? No, God is not indifferent to ungodliness and wrongdoing. The whole epistle distinguishes sharply between light and darkness (1 John 2:8), love and hatred (2:9-10), truth and lie (2:21), justice and unrighteousness, good and evil (3:12), God and devil (3:10), Christ and antichrist (2:22f.), life and death (2:25). It does not come as a surprise,

Charge: Giving and Forgiving in a Culture Stripped of Grace (Grand Rapids: Zondervan, 2006).

17. This is, I take it, the main thrust of the somewhat mysterious saying about the "mortal sin" about which one should not pray and about God's not giving life to those who commit it (1 John 5:16).

therefore, that just a few verses after our text St. John writes about God's *judgment* (4:17-18).

How is God's love related to God's judgment? God's love has different effects on people, depending on the basic orientation of their being and the moral character of their deeds. When we do what is right (basically, when we love), we experience God's love as delight and approval, as God's face "shining on us." When we do what is evil (basically, when we are indifferent or harm), we experience God's love as wrath and condemnation. Why wrath and condemnation? Not because God does not love us, but so that the loving God can return us to the good from which we have fallen.[18]

Whether God is angry with us or delights in us, whether God approves of us or condemns us, God loves us with the same unchanging divine love rooted in, and indeed identical with, the very being of God. That is why those who "remain in love" and thereby remain "in God" have "confidence" in the day of judgment and need not fear (4:17-18).

Identifying God

What are the consequences of the claim that God is love for the knowledge of God? One consequence is obvious: From a Christian point of view, those who do deny that God is love do not know God properly. Martin Luther was deeply concerned with rightly identifying the character of God as love; indeed, one can say that the whole of the Reformation was about the struggle over the proper understanding of God's character as love.

Luther resisted vigorously — sometimes overzealously, I might add — two *false* forms of "knowing" God, both of which, he believed, entailed denial that God is love. First is the straightforward belief that God is ill-disposed toward human beings as sinners, that God hates them on ac-

18. In the Christian tradition a distinction is often made between person and work: God loves the person, but not the work (if the work is sinful). Augustine puts the same idea, now applied to human love, this way: "Love not in the man his error, but the man: for the man God made, the error the man himself made. Love that which God made, love not that which the man himself made" (Homilies on 1 John, n. 11).

count of their sin. That cannot be true, because God is love. God cannot but love sinners and precisely because God loves them hate their sin. The second false opinion about God is that God is "favorably disposed toward me because of my efforts and works."[19] To come to God with one's noble deeds and good works expecting God's love in return is to commit three mistakes in one: (1) about human beings and their good deeds (by claiming as their possession what is in fact a gift from God); (2) about God's character (by denying God "is nothing but love"[20]); and (3) about God's love (by denying that God's love is such that it cannot be earned, that it comes utterly "without cost"[21]).

Even though Luther was a fierce proponent of the idea that unconditional love describes the very being of God, he still did not believe that those Jews and Muslims — not just fellow Catholic Christians — who disagreed with him on this point worshiped a false God. In his *Large Catechism* he insisted that Jews and Muslims do "believe in, and worship, only one true God," even if they do not "know what His mind towards them is,"[22] which is to say, even if they, according to his understanding of their faiths, do not believe that God's love toward them is utterly unconditional.[23] Those who deny that God is sheer love do not therefore worship a false God. Instead, they (partly) falsely describe the one true God. That was a grave enough problem for Luther — for not to believe and therefore not to trust that God is gracious to you is for you *not* to *have* a gracious God! But even he did not suggest that those who (like himself) affirm the unconditionality of God's love and those who deny the unconditionality of God's love (Catholics, Jews, and Muslims) therefore do not believe in the same God! That he did not do so is all the more surprising, given that his views of both Muslims and Jews were famously and very disturbingly negative.

19. Martin Luther, *Luther's Works,* 30:293.
20. Martin Luther, *Luther's Works,* 30:293.
21. Martin Luther, *Luther's Works,* 30:294.
22. Martin Luther, *Large Catechism* (Philadelphia: Muhlenberg, 1959), 63.
23. Notice that Luther did not believe that God's attitude of utterly unconditional love is limited to Christians. It extends to all people, even those who do not believe that God has such an attitude toward them. See Christoph Schwöbel, "The Same God? The Perspective of Faith, the Identity of God, Tolerance and Dialogue" (paper presented at God and Human Flourishing Consultation, Yale Center for Faith and Culture, New Haven, CT, 2009), 16.

OF GOD AND MAMMON

Knowing God — Loving Neighbor

The entire text of 1 John 4:7-12 assumes the importance of identifying the character of God rightly, but its main concern lies elsewhere — not in the way we think about God, but in the way we behave toward neighbors. "Everyone who loves is born of God and knows God" (v. 7), which implies that everyone who does not love neighbor is not born of God. Why does it not suffice to love God? The reason is simple: God's love is not a love that remains contained within the Godhead but flows out toward creatures. Any human love that would lay claim to being "from God" and like God's love must flow toward others, toward neighbors. A love simply returned to God is very much unlike divine love. Love passed on to the neighbor is like God's love. That is why everyone who is born of God loves, and everyone loves who is born of God. The point can be put tersely: no love of neighbor, no birth from God.

Similarly, no love of neighbor, no knowledge of God.[24] "Whoever does not love does not know God" (1 John 4:7). We can have accurate information about God, and we can also affirm as true all the accurate information about God we have, but still not know God. To know God it is not enough to give cognitive assent to truth about God; we must "do the truth" (1:6), we must act as God acts, be as God is (though, of course, always mindful of God's radical difference from creatures!). God is not known where neighbor is not loved. Knowledge of God is tied to affinity with God in who humans are and how they act.[25]

St. Augustine pushed the connection between love of neighbor and knowledge of God even a bit further. Commenting on verse 7 he wrote: "Whosoever therefore violates charity, let him say what he will with his

24. As Judith Lieu insists rightly in her fine commentary on 1 John, our text insists on "absolute nonnegotiability of love as the defining characteristic of those who would claim to know God" (Judith M. Lieu, *I, II, & III John: A Commentary* [Louisville: Westminster John Knox, 2008], 179).

25. This thought may be somewhat difficult. It may be made plausible if we reflect that one may not really know a person without in some sense participating in his or her projects. Max Scheler has plausibly advocated this idea. "The person of another can only be disclosed to me by my *joining in the performance* of his acts, either cognitively, by 'understanding' and vicarious 're-living,' or morally, by 'following in his footsteps' " (*The Nature of Sympathy* [trans. Peter Heath; Hamden, CT: Archon, 1970], 167).

tongue" — let him say all the right things about who Christ is and what the nature of God is — he still denies Christ and is therefore "an antichrist" and "acts against God."[26] Not to love neighbor is not just not to know God; it is actually to *deny* God. Clearly, Augustine believed, it is worse for concrete *deeds* toward neighbor to be misaligned with the character of God than for *thoughts* about God to be misaligned with the character of God. If Augustine is correct in this assessment, the consequences for Christians' relation to non-Christians are astounding: nonbelievers or adherents of another religion, if they love, can be closer to God than Christians notwithstanding Christians' formally correct *beliefs* about God or even explicit, outward faith in Jesus Christ![27]

This elevation of deeds above beliefs is the consequence of the claim that God is love. God loves, therefore we must love; God is love, therefore we must "be" love — delighting and correcting, supporting and resting, and at all times benevolent, beneficent, and actively caring love.

Coming to Know God

But how can one come to know God properly? How can one come to act as God acts and be as God is? "Beloved, let us love one another, because love is from God" (1 John 4:7).[28] At one level, coming to act as God acts is

---

26. Augustine, *Homilies* 7.2, p. 1180, and 7.5, p. 1183.

27. Raymond Brown correctly claims that "the author's negative statement (4:8a), 'One who does not love has known nothing of God,' places the secessionists (against whom it is aimed) on the same level as 'the Jews' of John 16:3 who 'never knew the Father' and as the world which 'never knew [recognized] God' (1 John 3:1e)" (*The Epistles of John* [Garden City, NY: Doubleday, 1982], 549). The statement in 4:8 is more general and applies more broadly than just to secessionists.

28. The command is directed to fellow believers and urges them to love one another. But this command is not simply a group-specific one. If God's love encompasses all, then all human beings are commanded to love, and they are commanded to love all human beings. This does not exclude the possibility that there can be group-specific and person-specific divine commands, a group's or individual's specific "callings." See Robert M. Adams, "Vocation," *Faith and Philosophy* 4/4 (1987): 448-63. See also Michael Wassenaar, "Four Types of Calling: The Ethics of Vocation in Kierkegaard, Brunner, Scheler and Barth" (Ph.D. diss., Yale University, 2009), 27-37.

a matter of obedience to a command. The statement I quoted is an exhortation — "let us" — but it has the force of a command (see 3:23). Love is from God, God is love; therefore we ought to love! The command, which concerns primarily actions, is appropriate, since indeed human beings ought to align themselves with those of their creator, in whose image they are made. But the command is also insufficient. It fails to give what those who are to love need the most — sufficient motivation and power actually to obey and to love.

"Beloved, since God loved us so much, we also ought to love one another" (1 John 4:11). At another and deeper level, coming to act as God acts is a matter of seeing who God is and how God has acted in loving humanity — immeasurably, unconditionally, universally, indiscriminately, forgivingly. God is a model of who human beings should be and how therefore they should act. This takes us back to Luther's concern: If we ought to be as God is, it matters that we identify rightly who God is — in particular, who God is toward us. Hence the pervasive concern with "right doctrine" in the epistle. Understanding properly who God is and how God loves us motivates us to love neighbors. At this second level, we come to know God in that we see, we are moved, and we seek to become like.

In the first and second ways of coming to know God — obedience to a command and imitation of an example — the relationship between God and us is an external one: we listen and obey, we observe and imitate. In the third way the relationship between God and us is more intimate — not one of spatial and temporal distance, but one of internal presence. It concerns both our being and our acting in their unity. "If we love one another, God lives in us," says our text (v. 12). A few verses later we read: "God is love, and those who abide in love abide in God, and God abides in them" (4:16). Indwelled by God, we are conformed to God and act like God. Having still in mind command and imitation as the first and second ways of doing the truth and being in the truth and so knowing God, we might be tempted to conclude that God will live in us *if* we show sufficient diligence in loving our neighbors. But that would be to turn things on their head. It would also make God's active love for us dependent on our love and therefore be to deny the gratuity of God's love and, in a sense, the very being of God.

Consider first that *all* love is "from God" (v. 7) — God is its ultimate source, not we ourselves or any creature. If we love, it is not because we have generated love ourselves, say, by deciding to imitate how God acts in Jesus Christ. If we love, it is only because God has somehow engendered love in us (say, by means of observing how God acted in Christ). Consider second that "God is love" (v. 8). When God gives love, God does not give something that God has, but something that God is. So the way God gives love is by giving God's very self. God comes to "live in us," as our text says (v. 12). Love of neighbor is not the condition of God's presence in us; God's presence in us is the condition of love of neighbor. Living in us, God shapes the very character of our selves so that we can be and act in conformity to God. Love of neighbor is a *sign* of God's presence — a sign more sure than any other. Where genuine love is, God is there.

Manifestations of God

Ordinary love between ordinary human beings is a visible manifestation of the invisible God! God, whom no one can see, can in fact be seen — if we know how and where to look. St. Augustine writes eloquently about proper and improper ways to "see" God:

> But let no man imagine God to himself according to the lust of his eyes. For so he makes unto himself either a huge form, or a certain incalculable magnitude which, like the light which he sees with the bodily eyes, he makes extend through all directions; field after field of space he gives it all the bigness he can; or, he represents to himself like as it were an old man of venerable form. None of these things do you imagine. There is something you may imagine, if you would see God; *God is love.* What sort of face has love? what form has it? what stature? what feet? what hands has it? no man can say. And yet it has feet, for these carry men to church: it has hands; for these reach forth to the poor: it has eyes; for thereby we consider the needy.[29]

When we encounter active love, when we give it and receive it, the invisible and unique God, who dwells in inapproachable light, becomes "visi-

---

29. Augustine, *Homilies* 7.10, p. 1186.

ble" in the world — visible not to the physical eye, not even to the intellectual eye, but visible to the spiritual eye.

For Christians, all manifestations of the One God in the ordinariness of neighborly love are strictly speaking but echoes of God's self-manifestation in Jesus Christ. "God's love was revealed among us in this way: God sent his only Son into the world so that we might live through him" (1 John 4:9). The verse parallels a fuller one at the beginning of St. John's Gospel: "No one has ever seen God. It is God the only Son, who is close to the Father's heart, who has made him known" (1:18). As Jesus Christ fed the hungry, healed the sick, embraced the children, feasted with the outcasts; as he announced the nearness of God and preached repentance; as he was crucified as God's Lamb bearing the sin of the world, and as he rose again — in all these acts of love God's love was present, and in his life, the God who is love, was fully made known.

Conclusion: Six Theses

For Christians:

1. God is love in God's very being apart from God's relation to creation;
2. God's love of creatures is an expression of God's being and is therefore always "first" and utterly unconditional;
3. We know that God is love and how God is through Jesus Christ, the unconditional love of God enacted in history;
4. We ought to love our neighbors in a way that echoes in our own creaturely way God's unconditional and universal love for humanity;
5. To know the God of love we must love neighbors, whoever these neighbors are;
6. For us to love, the God who is love and who creates and redeems humanity out of love must engender our love and love through us.

CHAPTER SIX

Hunger for Infinity: Christian Faith and the Dynamics of Economic Progress

A Cloak and a Cage

At the end of Max Weber's *The Protestant Ethic and the Spirit of Capitalism,* at the point where what its author calls "purely historical discussion" edges toward "the world of judgments of value and of faith," we read, "In Baxter's view the care for external goods should only lie on the shoulders of the 'saint like a light cloak, which can be thrown aside at any moment.' But fate decreed that the cloak should become an iron cage."[1] The intriguing questions about the nature of "fate" and its decree and about how it was carried out need not concern us here. Important for my purposes is the double irony entailed in the transformation of the "cloak" into the "cage."

---

1. Max Weber, *The Protestant Ethic and the Spirit of Capitalism* (trans. Talcott Parsons; 1904-5; New York: Charles Scribner's Sons, 1958), 181.

This chapter was originally prepared for a conference titled "Rethinking Materialism: Sociological and Theological Perspectives," held at the Center for the Study of American Religion, Princeton University, June 11-13, 1993. I am grateful for the assistance I received in preparing this paper from my students Robert Cahill and Telford Work. My friends the professors Philip Clayton, Judith Gundry, and James William McClendon Jr. read a draft of the essay and offered valuable advice. I benefited also from the discussion during the conference, especially from the comments by professors Neil Smelser, Nicholas Wolterstorff, and Robert Wuthnow.

The first irony was intentional. Richard Baxter, the old Puritan simpleton, thought mammon's yoke was easy and its burden light — provided one's heart was set on the things of God. But in fact the powers unleashed by transplanting asceticism "out of monastic cells into everyday life"[2] — and by a few other things, such as the changes in economic organization and social structures[3] — have proved stronger than the heart's desire to serve the one true master. The burden of care for external goods became heavy and the worldly saints weary; the light cloak turned into an iron cage. From behind the closed doors of the cage, Christ's call to come and find rest (Matt. 11:28-30) could be heard only as a faint echo from a distant past.

The obverse of Christ's offer of rest was the warning that one cannot serve both God and mammon (Matt. 6:24). For many in the seventeenth century and after, mammon seemed an increasingly attractive lord, however. In order to pursue the creation and enjoyment of wealth with a good conscience, one needed cleanly to separate the economic and religious spheres, treating them no longer "as successive stages within a larger unity, but as parallel and independent provinces, governed by different laws, judged by different standards, and amenable to different authorities."[4] This disjunctive maneuver was bound to render Christ's call and his command ineffectual in the economic sphere. When the maneuver succeeded, it seemed that the age of freedom had dawned. But as time went by, it became apparent that it was freedom to do what one wanted — in an iron cage. The "tremendous cosmos of the modern economic order" has come to determine "the lives of all individuals who are born into" it, "with irresistible force," wrote Weber.[5] He exaggerated. There are people who successfully resist the force of modern economic order. Yet most succumb while cheerfully believing that they are exercising the greatest of all freedoms: the freedom of the consumer. This irony

2. Weber, *The Protestant Ethic*, 158.

3. See Richard Henry Tawney's foreword in Weber, *The Protestant Ethic*, 1-11; Bob Goudzwaard, *Capitalism and Progress: A Diagnosis of Western Society* (trans. J. Van Nuis Zylstra; Grand Rapids: Eerdmans, 1978).

4. Richard Henry Tawney, *Religion and the Rise of Capitalism: A Historical Study* (New York: Harcourt, Brace & Company, 1926), 279.

5. Weber, *The Protestant Ethic*, 181.

is the second in the talk about the replacement of the light cloak by an iron cage, the one Weber does not seem to have intended.

The double irony illustrates well a fundamental *aporia* at the interface of religion and economic life in the modern age: the seeming powerlessness of religious moral appeals and the slavery of "material boys and girls" — what used to be called *homo oeconomicus* — to endless desires if they refuse to heed these appeals. Have we locked the door of the cage from the inside and misplaced the key? Before proceeding with a search, it might be good to ask some deceptively simple questions: Are we indeed in a cage? If we are, how have we gotten into it? Might our "gods" be partly to blame?

The questions I propose to address betray at the outset the relatively narrow focus of this essay. Various deeply disturbing aspects of contemporary economic life will remain outside its scope. For instance, I will say nothing about the injustice of people's finding themselves excluded from the basic means of livelihood. My silence does not come from a lack of concern.[6] In any case, the futility of acquisitive materialism I intend to tackle here is no less significant a problem than injustice. The two are closely interrelated: Where there is justice, there will be abundance even amid scarcity;[7] where there is contentment, justice will flow like a mighty river.

The Cage . . .

In his classic *The Affluent Society,* John Kenneth Galbraith compared the struggle in modern societies to satisfy their wants with "the efforts of the squirrel to keep abreast of the wheel that is propelled by his own efforts."[8] More recently, Juliet B. Schor joined him and deplored "capital-

6. See Miroslav Volf, *Zukunft der Arbeit — Arbeit der Zukunft: Der Arbeitsbegriff bei Karl Marx und seine theologische Wertung* (Munich: Kaiser, 1988); and Volf, *Work in the Spirit: Toward a Theology of Work* (New York: Oxford University Press, 1991).

7. See M. Douglas Meeks, *God the Economist: The Doctrine of God and Political Economy* (Minneapolis: Fortress, 1989), 157ff.

8. Kenneth John Galbraith, *The Affluent Society* (Boston: Houghton Mifflin, 1958), 154.

ism's squirrel cage": people are trapped in the endless "cycle of work-and-spend," whose poles mutually reinforce each other.[9]

Squirrel Cage

For Galbraith (and Schor), capitalist *production* is the culprit. Contrary to the widespread assumption that existing needs call for products to satisfy them, in modern capitalism the production "creates the wants the goods are presumed to satisfy." In other words, the production "fills a void that it has itself created."[10] Galbraith is largely correct. One must be a blind ideologue to embrace the idyllic image of producers as nothing more than zealous servants, alert to any discomfort of their masters, the consumers, and ready to give a helping hand — and justly receiving generous rewards for their deft assistance. At least since Hegel, social critics have not failed to note that the spiraling wants of consumers are partly contrived by profit-seeking producers.[11]

Although correct, Galbraith's diagnosis is partial. So is his proposed cure. It is futile simply to blame the producers, assuming that if their drive for profit could be tamed, then modern societies would have solved the problem of production and have freed themselves to "proceed . . . to the next task."[12] To get closer to the cure, we need to ponder why efforts at contriving wants are so easily crowned with success and why we never get around to the "next task." The answer lies not just in expert marketing but also in the character of human needs. As Kant pointed out in his *Critique of Judgment*, it is not human nature "to stop possessing and en-

9. See Juliet B. Schor, *The Overworked American: The Unexpected Decline of Leisure* (New York: Basic Books, 1992), 117-65.

10. Galbraith, *The Affluent Society*, 155, 153.

11. Georg Wilhelm Friedrich Hegel, *Grundlinien der Philosophie des Rechts oder Naturrecht und Staatswissenschaft im Grundrisse* (1821; Frankfurt a. M.: Suhrkamp, 1976), §191; see also Hegel, *Vorlesungen über Rechtsphilosophie* (ed. K. H. Itling; 1818-31; Stuttgart-Bad Canstatt: Frommann-Holzboog, 1973), 593; Karl Marx, *Grundrisse der Kritik der Politischen Ökonomie. Rohentwurf* (1857/58; Berlin: Dietz Verlag, 1974), 14.

12. Galbraith, *The Affluent Society*, 356.

joying at some point and be satisfied."[13] Insatiability belongs to the basic makeup of human beings.

Ought we not be cautious, however, with talk about insatiability? Does it not impose on us as fate the unceasing quest for material goods? Moreover, is not such talk a simpleminded and arrogant projection of modern possessive individualism and of the belief in unlimited progress onto human nature in general?[14] The alternative claim, that not all human beings have an insatiable appetite for goods and services, strikes us as plausible; many people seem content with what they have. How then can insatiability be rooted in human nature?

In a sense, however, the contentment of some people is beside the point. Just as it is true that there are content people in capitalistic societies, so it is also true that there have always been insatiable people in pre-capitalistic societies. The human race did not need to wait for capitalism to infect it with the virus of insatiability. If this metaphor is appropriate at all, then the virus was there all along. It was active in particular strata of society throughout history, until finally a general epidemic broke out with the rise of capitalism in the West. The inactive virus just needed a change in socioeconomic and cultural conditions to provide it a friendly environment. The immune system was weakened, and the insatiable appetite attacked anything it could find under the sun. The idea that the crapulousness bespoke a serious illness was suppressed.

Insatiability

As I shall argue shortly, *cultural acceptance,* even *encouragement,* of insatiability is unique to modernity. Insatiability itself is not. For proof of the latter, one has only to look at the strange world of the book of Ecclesiastes, a text I will engage throughout this chapter. Insatiability is its dominant theme. Consider the following image:

---

13. Kant, *Critique of Judgment* (trans. W. S. Pulhar; 1790; Indianapolis: Hackett, 1987), §83; see also Hegel, *Grundlinien der Philosophie*, §190.

14. See Gasiet Seev, *Menschliche Bedürfnisse: Eine theoretische Synthese* (Frankfurt a. M.: Campus Verlag, 1981), 43.

All streams run to the sea,
    but the sea is not full;
to the place where the streams flow,
    there they continue to flow.

(Eccles. 1:7; see also Prov. 30:15-16)

Just as the flow of the streams never fills the sea, so humans remain forever unsatiated, all their toil notwithstanding.[15] Ecclesiastes not only registers insatiability, however. The various concrete images the book employs also show a clear awareness of its rootedness in human nature.

The first cause of insatiability is human animality: "All human toil is for the mouth, yet the appetite is not satisfied" (6:7). To live as an animal being is to have needs and to require their perpetual satisfaction. One might object that this is not quite what we mean by insatiability. After all, how many meals can you have in one evening? We eat, and we are satisfied. Yet the hunger invariably recurs. The only thing that can break the cycle of hunger and satiation is death. Animal beings can be satiated *fully* but never *finally*.

Human insatiability proper is not a function of animality, however, but of spirituality. The author of Ecclesiastes writes,

. . . the eye is not satisfied with seeing,
    or the ear filled with hearing.

(Eccles. 1:8)

The human stomach can be satisfied — for the time being at least. But the human eye and ear are insatiable, forever eager to see and hear something new (as well as often wishing to revisit the old). One could object here, too, that a few hours spent at the Louvre and hearing Schubert's string quartet generally satisfy most Western art and music lovers. Yet if we know how to appreciate art, we will want return to the Louvre and to Schubert after we have taken a rest. We might also want to see

---

15. See Roland Edmund Murphy, *Ecclesiastes* (Word Biblical Commentary 23A; Waco: Word, 1992), 8. In the following I do not pretend to be *exegeting* select passages from Ecclesiastes. Rather, I look at the theological and philosophical insights that may lie behind Qoheleth's statements and above all at new vistas that may be opened by them.

some treasures from the Hermitage and listen to Mahler. Imagination and reflection forever carry the eye and the ear beyond the point of seeing and hearing, and create a void and the need for it to be filled; indeed, they make human beings want to see and hear "what no eye has seen, nor ear heard" (1 Cor. 2:9).

We can see why the eye has come to signify desire in Ecclesiastes (see Eccles. 2:10). Its restlessness is a case in point of the self-transcendence of human beings: they are always beyond every given situation.[16] And because they are, the experience of insatiability glides into the experience of the *tantalous*. Human beings are never satisfied because their desire is always already beyond any given object of their desire; they are reaching for what always eludes them. And so, as Ecclesiastes observes, people find no "end to all their toil, and their eyes are never satisfied with riches" (4:8).

Since human beings are social animals, self-transcendence takes place in a social setting. The eye sees, compares, and — envies. "Then I saw that all toil and all skill in work come from one person's envy of another" (4:4). As the one envies the other, rivalry goads each to outdo the other. The effort expended increases and proficiency is sharpened.[17] And that in turn reinforces insatiability.

Ecclesiastes' description of the dynamic of insatiability shows a striking resemblance to the dynamic of insatiability in modern societies, even if the "spirit of capitalism," which makes the pursuit of profit an end in itself, is absent from it.[18] Might this resemblance not illustrate its author's claim that "there is nothing new under the sun" (1:9) — a claim that strikes us as so outlandish in an age of innovation?

Whatever one might think of the presumed needs of an *infinite* being, Hegel was no doubt correct that being needful is an essential characteristic of a *finite* being.[19] Humans are finite beings, but the nature of

---

16. See Max Scheler, *Die Stellung des Menschen im Kosmos* (1928; Berlin: Vranke Verlag, 1978), 36ff.; Wolfhart Pannenberg, *Anthropologie in theologischer Perspektiv* (Göttingen: Vandenhoeck & Ruprecht, 1983), 40ff.

17. See Graham Ogden, *Qoheleth* (Sheffield: JSOT Press, 1987), 67.

18. See Karl Marx and Friedrich Engels, *Werke* (Berlin: Dietz Verlag, 1979), 22:144ff.

19. See Georg Wilhelm Friedrich Hegel, *Wissenschaft der Logik* (2 vols.; 1813; Hamburg: Verlag von Felix Meiner, 1963), 2:409; cf. Seev, *Menschliche Bedürfnisse*, 36.

their finitude makes their needs infinite. If we eliminated all the *contrived* wants generated by either helpful or greedy producers, the squirrel wheel would no doubt turn at a much slower pace, but it would not come to a halt. Consumerism is a creation of capitalism. Insatiability is not; capitalism only capitalizes on it.

The rootedness of insatiability in human nature leads to a very simple but fundamental insight: *the economic problem cannot be solved by economic means alone,* not even in a hundred years, as Keynes suggested in his frequently quoted essay titled "Economic Possibilities for Our Grandchildren."[20] Purely economic solutions to economic problems ignore the insatiability that keeps the squirrel wheel in motion — not only the insatiability of our hungry mouth and envious eye that seek "conveniences according to the nicety and delicacy of taste,"[21] but also the insatiability of the inner vision lured by the promise of perpetual progress.

. . . of Vanities

(1) "Among the many models of the good society no one has urged the squirrel wheel," noted Galbraith dryly.[22] His sarcasm is to the point. For in fact the notion of the good society that has dominated public imagination in the West for quite some time is not so far from the squirrel wheel. It disguises itself under a different name, however. We call it progress.

Progress

In one sense, faith in progress is dead. When two centuries ago Johann Gottlieb Fichte proclaimed that the true paradise was not a gift of grace that humanity enjoyed in the distant past, but a promised land to be con-

---

20. John Maynard Keynes, "Economic Possibilities for Our Grandchildren," in *Essays and Persuasions* (London: Macmillan, 1931), 366.

21. Adam Smith, *Lectures on Justice, Police, Revenues, and Arms* (ed. E. Cannan; Oxford: Clarendon, 1896), 160.

22. Galbraith, *The Affluent Society,* 159.

quered by humanity's efforts in the not-too-distant future,[23] he was not a lone voice crying in the wilderness. With many Western thinkers of the eighteenth and nineteenth centuries, he shared the belief that humanity was destined to build for itself "a paradise according to the blueprint of the one it lost" — with significant architectonic improvements, to be sure.[24] In the meantime, Westerners have learned through bitter lessons what they ought to have known without them: the scaffolding will never be removed from the construction site "Paradise"; even the price of pouring the foundation was much higher than anyone should have paid.

The hope of building a paradise has vanished, and with it a fixed destination for the spiral of needs. But faith in progress persists. This curiosity is easily explained when we consider that a utopian *destination* was never at the core of the idea of progress. As Christopher Lasch[25] has argued, central to the modern conception of progress is not so much "the promise of a secular utopia that would bring history to a happy ending but the promise of steady improvement with no foreseeable ending at all" (47). This notion of progress takes its cue from science as a "self-perpetuating inquiry" (48). It is predicated on two sets of beliefs. The one is the positive assessment of insatiability and of the proliferation of wants (13, 45), and the other an "expectation that the expansion of the productive forces can continue indefinitely" (39).

Insatiability and Progress

The awareness is growing that what we thought to be a road of perpetual progress is in fact a dead-end street. Like many before him, Lasch has underscored the ecological limits of growth (though criticizing at the same time "a very narrow ideal of the good life" [529] that faith in progress presupposes). He writes, "[The discovery that] the earth's ecology will no

---

23. Johann Gottlieb Fichte, *Sämmtliche Werke* (ed. I. H. Fichte; Berlin: Veit und Comp, 1845/46), 7:342.

24. Fichte, *Sämmtliche Werke*, 7:12; see also Volf, *Zukunft der Arbeit*, 32-33.

25. Christopher Lasch, *The True and Only Heaven: Progress and Its Critics* (New York: W. W. Norton, 1991). Subsequent page references are given parenthetically in the text.

longer sustain an indefinite expansion of productive forces deals the final blow to the belief in progress" (529). Others, such as Fred Hirsch,[26] have drawn attention to the social limits of growth. But even if there were no ecological and social limits to growth, would the pursuit of progress predicated on insatiability make sense?

On the one hand, progress seems inextricably tied to the positive assessment of insatiability — at least an indefinite progress does. Insatiability is the fuel that keeps the engine of progress going. Were people to become content, no progress would occur. At a deeper level, however, the association of progress and insatiability is oxymoronic. The notion of progress from which a final destination has been removed cannot imply that we are asymptotically approaching the goal — as, for instance, Kant's notion of moral progress assumes the approximation toward "the highest good possible on earth,"[27] or as scientific progress seems to entail an ideal explanation that is treated as true. Perfect goodness is desirable for Kant, and so is (arguably) an ideal explanation for a scientist; satiation is *undesirable* for modern believers in progress. At any moment on the time line of progress, humanity is equidistant from the goal for the simple reason that progress is not conceived as a terminal enterprise. This is what insatiability does to progress. In terms of satiation, the future only *seems* better than the present; the illusion is unmasked as soon as we compare the present with the past. Today we are exactly as satiated and exactly as unsatiated as we were yesterday.

Of course, progress *does* take place. Some additional wants get both created and satisfied, and there are new and more complex means of satisfying both old and new wants. Above all, we would rarely want to go back (even if we could), partly because life has been made easier through technological inventions, but partly also because of addiction to more recent goods and services.[28] *This* progress, however, never reaches below the surface. The level of satiation remains the same. As Paul L. Wachtel

26. Fred Hirsch, *The Social Limits to Growth* (Cambridge, Mass.: Harvard University Press, 1976).

27. Immanuel Kant, *Religion within the Limits of Reason Alone* (trans. T. M. Greene and H. H. Hudson; 1794; New York: Harper & Row, 1960), 126.

28. See Tibor Scitovsky, *The Joyless Economy: An Inquiry into Human Satisfaction and Consumer Dissatisfaction* (New York: Oxford University Press, 1976), 137.

writes, "We keep upping the ante. Our expectations keep accommodating to what we have attained. 'Enough' is just always over the horizon, and like the horizon it recedes as we approach it."[29] We eat but remain as hungry as ever. What can the progress mean if it takes place only at the surface? Does it consist in us being better and better — *unsatiated and insatiable?* A strange kind of progress indeed! If we thrive on insatiability, we might do well to rethink the ideology of progress — unless we are so fascinated with the movement at the surface that we forget about the lack of it in the depths.

What Is the Gain of the Gain?

The author of Ecclesiastes was not misled by surface currents. One might object that he was not sufficiently aware of them. After all, in his world there *was* nothing new under the sun (see Eccles. 1:9). Or was there? The conception that ancient societies were static is nothing more than a modern prejudice. Jacques Ellul rightly comments, "Progress did not take place then as fast as today, but it was just as basic for humanity's future." Moreover, Ecclesiastes does not seem to give a cyclical view of history; it does not "point out a cycle, an 'eternal return,' but a line of time punctuated by varying or comparable events."[30]

Important as the issue of the progress of humankind as a whole and its embeddedness in a philosophy of history is, it is not decisive for the problem we are discussing. Look at the *personal life* of the author of Ecclesiastes:

> I made great works; I built houses and planted vineyards. . . . I
> made myself gardens and parks, and planted in them all kinds of
> fruit trees. . . . I bought male and female slaves. . . . I also had great
> possessions of herds and flocks. . . . I also gathered for myself sil-
> ver and gold and the treasure of kings. . . . I got singers . . . and de-

29. Paul L. Wachtel, *The Poverty of Affluence: A Psychological Portrait of the American Way of Life* (New York: Free Press, 1983), 17.

30. Jacques Ellul, *Reason for Being: A Meditation on Ecclesiastes* (trans. Joyce Main Hanks; Grand Rapids: Eerdmans, 1990), 63, 66.

lights of the flesh, and many concubines. So I became great and surpassed all who were before me in Jerusalem. (2:4-5, 9)

This is "progress" by *our* definition. The talk about "surpassing" testifies that Ecclesiastes thought of it no differently.

What makes Ecclesiastes' author so different from a representative of modern Western culture is that in progress, he explained, "my wisdom remained with me" (2:9). At the very outset of the book, he posed the question our culture persistently refuses to ask: "What do people gain from all their toil at which they toil under the sun?" (1:3). He knew, of course, that hard work does bring gain, at least at the surface, and if one is lucky enough (see 9:11). The point of his question goes deeper, however. If work brings gain, *what is the gain of the gain?* This query calls to mind Jesus' rhetorical question: "For what will it profit them to gain the whole world and forfeit their life?" (Mark 8:36). A person who has only superficially read Jesus might ask, "But what if they *do not* forfeit their life? Could they then strive to gain the whole world?" Ecclesiastes' question pre-empts that kind of response. It asks in effect, "What will it profit a person to gain the whole world *even apart from the destiny of her soul?*" The answer comes as the conclusion of the list of his great accomplishments: "Then I considered all that my hands had done and the toil I had spent in doing it . . . and there was nothing to be gained under the sun" (2:11). After everything was gained, there comes a realization that there was nothing to be gained!

"Vanity of vanities . . . vanity of vanities! All is vanity" (1:2) reads the programmatic statement at the beginning of Ecclesiastes' treatise. Is this the frustrated cry of an overgorged overachiever fed up with life? Or did Ecclesiastes' author see something that seems veiled from most of us today? *"Nothing to be gained" is an inescapable corollary of insatiability.*

Uses of Pleasure

What about pleasure or happiness? No progress there? One would be hard-pressed to demonstrate that a person who is permanently overcoming a lack is happier than a person who does not feel a lack, that an insatiable person is happier than a content one. It is possible, of course, that a content person is suffering from myopia: she does not see that in the future she will be happier with more and better goods and services. This perspective might be correct if she is stricken with abject poverty. Above the line of abject poverty, however, better goods and services tend to contribute little to a sense of well-being. Happiness is notoriously difficult to measure, but none of the attempts to do so seem to confirm that the proliferation of wants and means to satisfy them entails progress in happiness.[31] Adam Smith, at any rate, believed that the "greater happiness" is a delusion — useful, though, to rouse and keep "in continual motion the industry of mankind."[32] To pursue happiness is a noble goal, but it too easily degenerates into an ideology that keeps us running in the squirrel wheel of vanities.

I am assuming that pleasure and happiness are good. And who would disagree? The author of Ecclesiastes certainly doesn't. His call to enjoyment resounds like a refrain throughout the book: "There is nothing better for mortals than to eat and drink, and find enjoyment in their toil" (2:24; see also 3:12-13, 22; 5:18; 8:15; 9:7). Yet as he has dared to take a close look at the meaning of work, so also he dares to examine pleasure without shying away from disturbing questions. "I said to myself, 'Come now, I will make a test of pleasure; enjoy yourself.' But again, this also was vanity. I said of laughter, 'It is mad,' and of pleasure, 'What use is it?'" (2:1-2). As is clear from the verses that follow (2:4-8), Ecclesiastes is talking not about mindless pleasures but about the joys "understood as the good life."[33] What is the use of *such* pleasures? The question strikes us as strange; the one who poses it seems not to know how to use the word "pleasure." But if the obvious answer to the strange question about the use of pleasure is "pleasure," the counter-answer must surely be "vanity." For pleasure is either a motif in the larger picture of a meaningful life, or it is itself meaningless.

John Stuart Mill insisted that it is better to be a dissatisfied Socrates than a satisfied pig. The claim might be true; I certainly would not dis-

---

31. See Wachtel, *The Poverty of Affluence,* 37ff.

32. Smith, in Michael Ignatieff, *The Needs of Strangers: An Essay on Privacy, Solidarity, and the Politics of Being Human* (New York: Penguin, 1986), 111.

33. Murphy, *Ecclesiastes,* 17.

pute it. But within the tradition that defines good as "what has an apt-
ness to produce pleasure in us" and evil as "what is apt to produce pain
in us,"[34] what good reasons can be given for Mill's claim?[35] Indeed, what
good reasons can be given for the claim that it is better to be a *satisfied*
Socrates than a satisfied pig — except that the one making the claim
happens to be not a pig but a human being? Just like any decent pig, a
self-satisfied modern Socrates who did not bother to learn anything
from his old namesake's reflection on happiness and self-control would
be enslaved in the cage of his vain pleasures.

God in the Cage

Taking God seriously, Richard Baxter thought, ought to have prevented
the light cloak of care for external goods from turning into an iron cage.
It did not. Moreover, a good argument has been made for God's complicity in the construction of the cage.[36]

Complicity of "God"

Attempts to strengthen this indictment of God have so far been unsuc-
cessful. Max Weber, who was the first to talk of God's complicity, claimed
only this much. More significant than a role God has played seems to

---

34. John Locke, *An Essay Concerning Human Understanding* (ed. A. C. Fraser; 2 vols.;
1690; Oxford: Clarendon, 1894), 1:340.

35. See Alasdair MacIntyre, *After Virtue: A Study in Moral Theory* (2d ed.; Notre
Dame: University of Notre Dame Press, 1984), 62ff.

36. See Weber, *The Protestant Ethic;* Troeltsch, *Protestantism and Progress: The Significance of Protestantism for the Rise of the Modern World* (1911; Philadelphia: Fortress,
1986), 70ff.; for discussions, see Robert W. Green, ed., *Protestantism and Capitalism: The
Weber Thesis and Its Critics* (Problems in European Civilization series; Boston: D. C.
Heath, 1959); Gordon Marshall, *In Search of the Spirit of Capitalism: An Essay on Max
Weber's Protestant Ethic Thesis* (New York: Columbia University Press, 1982). "The cage"
is not synonymous with capitalism, but stands for the self-enclosed world of *homo
oeconomicus* — whether in its pre-capitalist, pure capitalist, welfare-capitalist, or com-
munist form, or some possible post-capitalist form.

have been the creation of an economic system in which any non-profit-making enterprise would be doomed to extinction.[37] Yet God cannot be completely exonerated. God's demand for "intra-mundane asceticism" helped in the creation of the cage.

This new breed of asceticism consisted of two simple religious tenets that reinforced each other: labor must be performed with rigorous discipline since it is a calling from God, and all spontaneous enjoyment of the fruits of one's labor should be avoided. This attitude toward work and possessions, which is "irrational from the standpoint of purely eudaemonistic self-interest,"[38] contributed to the formation of the modern economic order that today powerfully shapes our lives.[39]

Initially God's complicity in the construction of the cage was unwitting; the contribution was "only an indirect and consequently involuntary one."[40] During the construction, God remained partly outside. Even if the prohibition of luxury made the so-called original accumulation[41] possible and hence stimulated the emergence of a capitalist economic system, it still reminded people that there was a world outside the cage that ought to impinge on what was going on inside. By highlighting the instances when the world and heaven were at odds, God's command underscored that the two belonged together. Even if the effectiveness of the command was rapidly diminishing, it still served as a reminder that the religious and economic aspects of life are interdependent components of a larger unity, not "independent provinces, governed by different laws."[42]

Over time the outside voice was silenced; God was drawn into the cage. Here I do not need to tell the whole fascinating — and ultimately pathetic — story of how God was entrapped and, like some blinded Samson, made to grind at the mill in the prison-house of the modern Philistines. The key element in this sacrilegious conspiracy was to recon-

---

37. See Weber, *The Protestant Ethic*, 91, 17.

38. Weber, *The Protestant Ethic*, 78.

39. See Ernst Troeltsch, *The Social Teaching of the Christian Churches* (trans. O. Wyon; 2 vols.; 1911; London: George Allen & Unwin, 1950), 645-46.

40. Troeltsch, *Protestantism and Progress*, 74.

41. See Marx and Engels, *Werke*, 23:741ff.

42. Tawney, *Religion and the Rise of Capitalism*, 279.

figure the basic sentiments about morality, prosperity, and historical development.[43] In his *Enquiry Concerning the Principles of Morals* (1927), David Hume put moral alternatives well:

> Luxury, or a refinement on the pleasures and conveniences of life, had long been supposed the source of every corruption in government, and the immediate cause of faction, sedition, civil wars, and the total loss of liberty. It was, therefore, universally regarded as a vice, and was an object of declamation to all satirists, and severe moralists. Those who prove, or attempt to prove, that such refinements rather tend to the increase of industry, civility, and arts regulate anew our *moral* as well as *political* sentiments, and represent, as laudable or innocent, what had formerly been regarded as pernicious and blameable.[44]

Hume's contrast between two kinds of moral and political sentiments recalls a contrast set up by Thomas Fuller in 1648 in a sermon on contentment: "Here we have two contrary opinions set on foot together, gain is godliness, says the worldling, whose Gold is his god, looking and telling thereof his saying of his prayers. *Godliness is great gain,* says God himself, by the mouth of the Apostle."[45] The "worldling" and a secularized version of his creed gained the upper hand; reconfiguration of moral sentiments largely succeeded. If earlier a person of virtue was a person of few needs, now endless wants became the key not only to success of industry but also to progress in civility. Insatiability was embraced, not bemoaned. The brakes were off, and the squirrel wheel started gaining momentum.

The so-called secularizing effects of wealth are proverbial. It cannot suffer a god beside itself. Yet God seems to dwell quite comfortably in the cage, even making a modest contribution to the business at hand, though occasionally plagued with bouts of (well-grounded?) fear of redundancy. It is for sociologists to analyze the multiple uses to which God

43. See M. M. Goldsmith, "Regulating Anew the Moral and Political Sentiments of Mankind: Bernard Mandeville and the Scottish Enlightenment," *Journal of the History of Ideas* 49 (1988): 587-606.

44. David Hume, *Enquiries Concerning Human Understanding and Concerning the Principles of Morals* (ed. L. A. Selby-Bigge; 1777; Oxford: Clarendon, 1927), 181.

45. Thomas Fuller, *A Sermon of Contentment* (London, 1648), 3-4.

has been put in the cage.[46] I want to draw attention here to what I perceive to be a major shift in the function of God in economic life *as reflected in popular theological discourse.*

God's New Job Description

The God who helped build the cage demanded ascetic denial of one's desires. One was to be content in consumption and disciplined in work (which, as Hegel pointed out, can be understood as "deferred desire"[47]). This is what it meant to practice one's work as a divine calling. In the post-Protestant age, influential thinkers counsel "re-appropriation of the idea of vocation,"[48] though they seem less interested in discipline and contentment than in working for the common good. But strong currents in popular religion want none of the old Protestant work ethic, their solemn declarations to the contrary notwithstanding. A case in point: the neo-charismatic preachers of the "prosperity gospel."[49] One could mention also the New Age movement and its relation to the business community.[50]

If one is to believe Tocqueville, it was never easy to ascertain from the discourses of American popular preachers "whether the principal object of religion is to procure eternal felicity in the other world, or prosperity in this."[51] I am not about to decide the issue. I am rather interested

46. See Robert Wuthnow, "Pious Materialism: How Americans View Faith and Money," *Christian Century,* 3 March 1993, 238-42.

47. Georg Wilhelm Friedrich Hegel, *Phänomenologie des Geistes* (1807; Frankfurt a. M.: Suhrkamp, 1977), 153.

48. Robert N. Bellah et al., *Habits of the Heart: Individualism and Commitment in American Life* (Berkeley and Los Angeles: University of California Press, 1985), 287; Bellah et al., *The Good Society* (New York: Knopf, 1991), 106-7.

49. See Kenneth Copeland, *The Laws of Prosperity* (Fort Worth, Tex.: Kenneth Copeland Publications, 1974); Gloria Copeland, *God's Will Is Prosperity* (Tulsa: Harrison House, 1978); John Avanzini, *The Wealth of the World: The Proven Wealth Transfer System* (Tulsa: Harrison House, 1989).

50. See David Gerschon and Gail Straub, *Empowerment: The Art of Creating Your Life as You Want It* (New York: Dell, 1989).

51. Alexis de Tocqueville, *Democracy in America* (trans. Phillips Bradley and Henry Reeve; 2 vols.; New York: Vintage Books, 1945), 2:135.

in what some of today's popular preachers say about *how* religious sentiments are to be employed in procuring prosperity.

In the book entitled *The Wealth of the World*, popular neo-charismatic preacher John Avanzini talks about "the battle of containment," or contentment.[52] But it is not a battle of the saints struggling to be content in a luring world; it is rather an unholy battle of the saints against Satan, who is seducing them through false religion into believing that they have enough (see 16). Satan needs to be resisted, however, for God wants the saints "to have exceedingly abundantly more than enough" so that they can have "all . . . needs and wants met" (125). In addition to faithful tithing and "generous offerings" (161), a sure weapon to defeat Satan is the following prayer: "No, you can't take any more of the money God intends for me. You can't keep me from the riches God intends for me to control for Him" (157).

This combative prayer tips us off as to how Christians ought to get hold of all the money God intends for them. Disciplined work is *not* the key. Rather, one needs to acquire "violent spiritual force" (21), "great quantities" of it (18): "God gives you the supernatural power to get wealth, power that goes beyond your natural abilities . . . not in some distant future life, but right now, in this life!" (114). And how does one access wealth with spiritual power? As the subtitle of the book — *The Proven Wealth Transfer System* — indicates, wealth gets *transferred* from the wicked to the saints. Avanzini writes, "God is going to literally confiscate the gold, silver, the stocks, the bonds, virtually every form of wealth that the wicked possess and *in these last days, transfer that wealth to the 'just' (dedicated, informed, committed Christians)*" (10-11). The religious purpose of the transfer is "to properly and abundantly fund the final events in His endtime plan" (10). That comes, however, only after all the needs and wants of the saints have been met.

I mention Avanzini's bizarre theology of wealth not because I believe religion will deliver what he promises. Avanzini's ideology serves, rather,

---

52. Avanzini, *The Wealth of the World*, 15. Subsequent page references are given parenthetically in the text. In contrast, read what the widely read Christian classic from the end of the seventeenth century, *The Pilgrim's Progress*, has to say about acquisition of wealth. It treats it as passage through a town called Vanity Fair (John Bunyan, *The Pilgrim's Progress*, Part One, Sixth Stage).

as an illustration of the radical change in the way Christian faith is supposed to relate to economic life. The God of the Puritans was a stern ascetic who inculcated discipline and demanded contentment — or at least it is those aspects of the personality of their God that have shaped the economic history of the West most significantly; the God of the prosperity preachers is a bon vivant who promises empowerment and abundance, along with the healing of wounds that the rough life of the market inflicts. Though not without a good deal of foot-dragging, the first God helped create the squirrel cage of vanities; with the zeal of a convert, the second God wants people to have fun in it and tries to facilitate its smooth turning as much as God can.

A change in God's job description could have been foreseen. To give the merry-go-round of vanities an initial push, one needed accumulation and therefore contentment. To keep it going, one needs spending. "If you want to have more cake tomorrow, you have to eat more today."[53] This is the magic paradox of wealth creation. Since a reluctant buyer needed to be replaced by an obsessive shopper, the God who demanded asceticism needed to give way to the God who encouraged self-indulgence. Furthermore, the God who commanded disciplined work had become expendable; the inner forces of the economic system itself were exacting discipline much more efficiently than God ever could. You can resist God with impunity — or so it seems; capitalism, however, punishes promptly and implacably.

In the meantime, however, skill and insight have become much more important than hard work or even talent. As Robert B. Reich has argued, in the modern economy the emphasis has shifted "from high volume to high value."[54] As a consequence, "symbolic-analytic" services, which include "problem-solving, problem-identifying, and strategic-brokering activities" and for which "creative use of knowledge" is central[55] overshadowed in importance routine production and in-person services. And that created a new market niche for God. As George Gilder puts it in "The Necessity of Faith," the last chapter in his book entitled *Wealth and*

53. Hobson, in Robert B. Reich, *The Work of Nations: Preparing Ourselves for Twenty-First-Century Capitalism* (1991; New York: Alfred A. Knopf, 1992), 45.

54. Reich, *The Work of Nations,* 81ff.

55. Reich, *The Work of Nations,* 177, 182. See also Volf, *Work in the Spirit,* 27ff.

Poverty, "Our greatest and only resource is the miracle of human creativity in a relation of openness to the divine."[56] From now on, God will empower and inspire creators of high value and periodically relieve overdoses of stress. High performers will not suffer divine moralizing, but they are superstitious enough to believe that they can use a bit of theurgy and religious therapy.

The End of False Gods

Who are the gods I dare to talk about in such an irreverent manner? Should I not rather be talking about religious *beliefs* — false religious beliefs, for that matter? But what is the difference between a false religious belief and an idol, except that one is *in* your head and the other also *outside* it? Christians who find themselves protesting against my insolence would insist that one god or the other — depending on the camp he comes from — was none other than the God of Jesus Christ. In response I would not deny some resemblance, but would underscore that the difference is glaring. Masters of subtle religious ideological manipulation engineered a gradual metamorphosis of the God of Jesus Christ into the god of this world. They were shrewd enough not to overdo it, however. The mask of the old God was retained; appearances must be kept up, you know.

The subtlety of the metamorphic solution might be new. The project of discarding uncomfortable gods is old. Consider Deuteronomic warnings for Israel not to forget the Lord their God who brought them out of the land of Egypt: "When you have eaten your fill and have built fine houses and live in them, and when your herds and flocks have multiplied, and your silver and gold is multiplied, and all that you have is multiplied, then do not exalt yourself, forgetting the Lord your God" (Deut. 8:12-14).

If a person is religious, when he forgets the one true God he will not simply develop a "self-made-man"-style faith with the simple credo, "My power and the might of my own hand have gotten me this wealth" (Deut.

56. George Gilder, *Wealth and Poverty* (New York: Bentham Books, 1981), 314.

8:17); he will also "follow other gods to serve and worship them" (8:19) — gods that, like the Baal of old, promise to do marvels in stimulating infinite growth and creating boundless prosperity. If not carefully attended to, wealth develops occult powers that erase memories of the one true God and generate new gods that are more congenial to its well-being.

What is good for wealth might not be good for its owners, however. Deuteronomy 8 ends with a threat of judgment to those who run after the gods whose only function is to bless insatiability and all the means to play up to it: ". . . so shall you perish" (v. 20). The cage will self-destruct and its gods will perish with it. For all their iron grip on the lives of people, both the cage and its gods are "like grass" and all their "glory like the flower of grass" (1 Peter 1:24).

Unlocking the Door

Here is the predicament of the God *in* the cage: If God rebels, God gets discarded; if God does not rebel, God gets co-opted; other less stark options are combinations of these two. I have no scruples about siding with a discarded God; rather, I have qualms about co-opting God myself. A discarded God might have lost usefulness for some people or even whole cultures; a co-opted God has lost divine dignity. One *ought not* have any use for a God without dignity. A God *with* dignity, on the other hand, might be of some benefit even to those who know no better than to want to discard that God. God's dignity can be preserved only if God steps outside the cage. Outside it is, of course, where the true God was all along; caught in the predicament inside the cage were the idols of this world.

A New Vision

The Voice from the outside said to the prophet Isaiah, "Cry out!" Perplexed, the prophet asked, "What shall I cry?" The Voice responded,

All people are grass,
their constancy is like the flower of the field. . . .

The grass withers, the flower fades;
  but the word of our God will stand forever.

(Isa. 40:6, 8)

In the previous sections I was concerned mainly with the fading of the flower. Here I want to look briefly at what the abiding word of God might have to say to our withering world. My direct interest is not to reconfigure our moral sentiments and reformulate our moral duties but to reshape our vision of the good life.

In the search for escape from the cage, I will look at some aspects of human work and consumption (in the broadest sense) and ask about their relation to religious commitments.[57] I am well aware that the cage, at least in its capitalist form, consists of much more than just attitudes and practices relating to work and consumption; it has powerful institutions and a corporate culture. The suggestions that I will make below cry out for structural underpinning. I will have to leave it to others, however, to look for possible alternatives to the present economic system (or, more precisely, for its structural improvements, for, if past experience is any guide, attempts at replacing the capitalist economic system are likely to produce worse forms of slavery). But whether we work on the institutional or the personal aspects of the problem, our task is essentially one, for the "spirit of the cage" is but one. It is totalitarian in intent too. Yet people do resist, with greater or lesser success; the cage never manages to be as nasty as it would want to be. Its inability to break down the spirit of opposition gives hope for a serene rebellion, at least on the part of a small but spirited resistance movement.

For a sufficiently disgruntled inhabitant of the cage, two simple solutions seem tempting. The first is the flight of the soul from the contingencies of the material world to the eternal and unchanging world of the Divine, to the spiritual heights of the Father in heaven. The second is the flight of the flesh-and-blood human being from the vicissitudes of the historical world to the stable cycle of nature, to the life-giving womb of "mother earth." The problem with both solutions is that one can never

---

57. In the following I am drawing on more extended discussion in my two books *Zukunft der Arbeit* and *Work in the Spirit*, while at the same time developing further some aspects of that discussion.

carry them far enough to be successful. They run counter to some stubborn features of human nature. Since we are not naked souls, our bodies in the end always triumph over any attempts at completely spurning materiality; the umbilical cord connecting us to the earth cannot be cut. But since we are not merely animal beings, our spirits always rebel against being confined to the world of pure nature; we must separate from "mother earth" and create a culture. Any viable alternative vision of the good life will have to take seriously not only God and environment but also *culture* — the world of human work and its fruits.[58]

Work

At first sight it might seem that in the cage one takes work too seriously. The Puritans were called to work by God and motivated by heavenly rewards; we are forced to work and lured to it by earthly recompenses. They worked hard; we work even harder.[59] On reflection, however, it becomes clear that the problem with the cage is exactly the opposite: it *does not take work seriously enough.* Work itself is not important; what matters is that goods get produced and money put into the pocket. The less one needs to work, the better. To borrow a phrase from Horace Bushnell, the cage is hard "at work to get rid of work."[60] Its view of work is purely instrumental. As Adam Smith expressed it, consumption is "the sole end and purpose of production."[61]

To free ourselves from captivity to the cage, we need to discover the *intrinsic value of work.* As the Genesis accounts of creation suggest, work is a fundamental dimension of human existence.[62] Work is not merely a means to life but one aspect of life. Luther and Calvin were therefore right to insist not only that human beings were originally created to

58. See James W. McClendon Jr., *Ethics: Systematic Theology* (1986; Nashville: Abingdon, 1989), 93ff.

59. See Schor, *The Overworked American.*

60. Horace Bushnell, *Work and Play* (New York: Charles Scribner's Sons, 1883), 22.

61. Adam Smith, *An Inquiry into the Nature and Causes of the Wealth of Nations* (1776; New York: Random House, 1937), 625.

62. See Volf, *Work in the Spirit,* 124-33.

work but also that God intended them to work "without inconvenience" and, "as it were, in play and with the greatest delight."[63] If work is to have full human dignity, it must be important not simply as a necessary means of earning; it must also be significant *as* work. The more work is its own reward, the more human dignity it will have.

But doesn't stressing the intrinsic value of work play into the hands of the cage? Won't it make the squirrel wheel spin even faster? No. It will actually slow it down. If work has intrinsic value, one will resist the pressure to produce frantically and instead take time to delight in work. In order to guard the dignity of the worker and subvert the dominance of the cage, we need to replace a production-oriented concept of work with "a *work-oriented* concept of work."[64]

A producer in the cage is interested in production mainly because she is interested in the profit or a paycheck. As it happens, one cannot make profit without a product; consumers may sometimes be blockheads, but they cannot be persuaded to give something for nothing. Hence a producer must be indirectly interested in the product too. But a worker who cares about what she is producing only enough to ensure that consumers are willing to purchase it is not likely to enjoy her work. Henri de Man rightly spoke of the "instinct" for the finished product, which is a presupposition for enjoyment of work.[65] Every good worker is something of an artist, not only enjoying what she does but also taking pride in what she has created. Paradoxical as it might sound, a work-oriented concept of work requires a *product-oriented* concept of work. If the worker does not psychologically own both the process of work and the product of work, production offends human dignity, irrespective of how high the profits or how large the paycheck may be.

63. Martin Luther, *D. Martin Luthers Werke. Kritische Gesamtausgabe* (Weimar: Böhlau, 1883), 42:78; see also John Calvin, *Commentaries on the First Book of Moses Called Genesis* (trans. John King; Grand Rapids: Eerdmans, 1948), 125.

64. Jürgen Moltmann, "The Right to Meaningful Work," in *On Human Dignity: Political Theology and Ethics* (trans. M. Douglas Meeks; Philadelphia: Fortress, 1984), 56; see also Robert K. Johnston, *The Christian at Play* (Grand Rapids: Eerdmans, 1983), 136-37.

65. Henri de Man, *Joy in Work* (London: George Allen & Unwin, 1929), 39.

66. See Schor, *The Overworked American*, 112.

Realm of Freedom

The cage is defined today not only by fascination with efficiency in production but also by obsessive *consumption;* the two constitute a mutually reinforcing and powerful work-and-spend syndrome.[66] The cure for the syndrome cannot be found in the "light cloak" therapy of the kind Baxter suggested. For one, the therapy has never worked. Moreover, it is bad for the patient. It aggravates the existing condition, and it has serious negative side-effects. The therapy is supposed to work by combining a positive assessment of the sustained outward pursuit of wealth with the requirement of inner detachment from it. But stress on unlimited economic growth is precisely the problem with the cage. The cure can consist only in finding ways to limit growth. If the positive assessment of the pursuit of wealth takes wealth too seriously, the requirement of inner detachment from it does not take it seriously enough. The readiness at any moment to throw aside the cloak of the care for external goods assumes tacitly that the soul *can* take flight from the material world to the spheres of pure spirit. As someone has noted, only those who merely work but do not nurture life could have come up with the idea of "the light cloak"; at *no* moment can the cloak be thrown aside without falling onto somebody else's shoulders. It has to be carried — and that is not only our fate but also our privilege. The question is, how do we keep the cloak from turning into the cage?

The answer does not lie in setting up some new version of the old distinction between necessities and luxuries that disregards the dynamic character of human needs. Rather, we should embed the valid care for external goods in the larger framework of what I have elsewhere called fundamental human needs: the need for enjoyment of God's creation, for the exercise and development of personal capacities, for cultivation of communion with our close and distant neighbors, and for the need to delight in God. All four of these closely interrelated needs coalesce in the single need for the new creation as the realm of freedom. As I wrote on this need in *Work in the Spirit:*

67. Volf, *Work in the Spirit,* 154.

In relation to the *need for God,* the realm of freedom is a realm of perfect fellowship with God, of seeing "face to face" and of understanding as fully as one is "fully understood" (1 Cor 13:12). In relation to the need for *solidarity with nature,* it is the realm of peace between human beings and nature liberated from corruptibility and the realm in which human beings jointly participate with nature in God's glory (Rom 8:19ff.; Isa 11:6f.; 65:25). In relation to the *need for fellow human beings,* it is the realm of unadulterated fellowship with one another, of pure "love, which binds everything together in perfect harmony" (Col 3:14). In relation to the *need for personal development,* it is the realm in which life is "realized only to be opened up to as yet unrealized possibilities" (Jüngel).[67]

The realm of freedom is an eschatological vision of the good life. This vision is the broadest framework in which we ought to place the creation of wealth and the satisfaction of dynamic needs for external goods. The more our production and consumer choices are guided by this vision rather than simply by our private satisfaction, the more humane they will be.[68]

God's Delight — Delight in God

Although the God I am talking about might not be sufficiently committed to efficiency and productivity to be useful to the cage, this God delights in good work. From Genesis 1 and 2 we learn that work "belongs to the very purpose for which God originally made" human beings.[69] Correspondingly, the Spirit of God calls and inspires people to use their abilities in doing good work in anticipation of God's new creation. Any remnants of the notion that, apart from keeping the worker's body and soul together, the only significance of work lies in the exercise it provides for our spiritual muscles ought to be discarded.

The God who inspires good work ensures that none of it will be ulti-

---

68. See M. Douglas Meeks, *God the Economist: The Doctrine of God and Political Economy* (Minneapolis: Fortress, 1989), 157ff.

69. Martin Hengel, "Arbeit im frühen Christentum," *Theologische Beiträge* 17 (1986): 179.

mately wasted. Without God, all human work has "the life span of a sand castle at the ocean's edge":[70] the worker and his work will ultimately dissolve into the thin vapor of vanity; even their memory will be erased (see Eccles. 2:12-17; 3:18-21). With God, however, all good work — everything good, true, and beautiful that human beings create — will be eternally preserved.[71] "God seeks out what has gone by," reads an obscure passage in Ecclesiastes (3:15b). Could the idea be that "nothing that the slippage of time drives away is lost,"[72] that "God gathers up forgotten time, lost works, all that has taken flight"?[73]

Life in the cage is predicated on insatiability. The cage perceives correctly that human "wants cannot be satiated,"[74] but it resists the notion that striving to satisfy them by economic means only encloses human beings into a circle of what Hegel called "false infinity."[75] The only proper "object" of human insatiability is the mystery of the infinite God. As Karl Rahner points out, the supreme act of knowledge of God "is not the abolition or diminution of the mystery but its final assertion."[76] Every act of knowing God both satisfies and engenders human curiosity; every encounter with God both quenches and deepens human thirst. In the infinite being of God, the incessant movement of the human spirit begins to arrive at its final rest.

How different is the endless exploration of the mystery of God from the futility of the earthly progress predicated on insatiability? How different are the divine quenching and deepening of human thirst from the cage's satisfying and creating of wants? As different as the heavens are from the earth! But why then should we not call the encounter between

---

70. John C. Haughey, *Converting Nine to Five: A Spirituality of Daily Work* (New York: Crossroad, 1989), 99.

71. See Volf, *Work in the Spirit*, 88-102; Haughey, *Converting Nine to Five*, 99-115.

72. Norbert Lohfink, *Koheleth* (Berlin: Echter Verlag, 1980), 33.

73. Ellul, *Reason for Being*, 68.

74. Lester Thurow, *The Zero-Sum Society* (New York: Basic Books, 1980), 120.

75. Hegel, *Grundlinien der Philosophie*, §185.

76. Karl Rahner, "The Concept of Mystery in Catholic Theology," in *Theological Investigations* (trans. K. Smyth; vol. 5; Baltimore: Helicon, 1966), 40; see also Eberhard Jüngel, *Gott als Geheimnis der Welt. Zur Begründung der Theologie des Gekreuzigten im Streit zwischen Theismus und Atheismus* (Tübingen: J. C. B. Mohr [Paul Siebeck], 1978), 341.

the inexhaustible God and the insatiable human being a *heavenly* cage of vanities? Because human beings are made to find ultimate fulfillment in the mystery of God. The cage thrives because it capitalizes on our longings for the inexhaustible God. It could be that we project our worldly ideals onto God, as Feuerbach argued.[77] God's infinity would then be the reverse side of human insatiability.[78] But I rather suspect that we are involved in an inverse projection by which we infuse the works of our own hands with the ability to satisfy our hunger for infinity. The endless stream of new goods and services has become a cornucopia of mystery, protection, and salvation. We call it progress. But its real name is *prayer.*[79]

"What do they not know, who know him who knows all things?" asked Saint Gregory rhetorically. Thomas Aquinas used the idea to argue "that those who see the divine substance do see all things."[80] If Aquinas is correct, then it should be legitimate to modify Gregory's question to read, "What do they not enjoy who enjoy God, who makes all things new?" Because God does not desire to be without the created world, because God gathers all lost works, the enjoyment of God cannot be a purely "spiritual," worldless enjoyment. It may seem that in turning to the mystery of God, we turn our backs to the whole created world of the good, the true, and the beautiful. In fact, when we turn to God, we find that same world in God, sanctified and glorified.

In God, in whom nothing worth preserving is lost, everything worth enjoying can be enjoyed.

77. Ludwig Feuerbach, *The Essence of Christianity* (trans. G. Eliot; 1841; New York: Harper & Row, 1957).

78. Meeks, *God the Economist*, 168.

79. So Irvin D. Yalom, *When Nietzsche Wept: A Novel of Obsession* (New York: Basic Books, 1992), 233, of love.

80. Thomas Aquinas, *Summa Contra Gentiles* (trans. Vernon J. Bourke; Notre Dame: University of Notre Dame Press, 1975), III/I, 196-97.

Afterword

—⚬⚬⚬—

My theological engagement with the Bible almost coincides with my career as a student and teacher of theology. My first published scholarly text, written while I was still a student at Fuller Theological Seminary, was a theological reading of 1 Corinthians 1:18-25. In the mid to late eighties, as an editor of the Croatian monthly *Izvori,* I wrote many more general-audience texts, which were basically engagements with scriptural texts. The essays in this volume continue that same trajectory.

Except for the first chapter, which was composed for this volume, I have written the remainder of the essays over a period of some sixteen years. Many people have helped me in the process — as research assistants, as dialogue partners, as participants at various conferences at which almost all the essays were originally presented. I thank all these people, though they are too numerous to mention here. Two people deserve special mention in conjunction with this volume. One is Jon Pott, the wise and witty Vice President and Editor-in-Chief of Eerdmans Publishing Company, who kindly agreed to publish the collection. The other is Connie Gundry Tappy, an able editor, who put the essays together and gave them editorial unity.

I dedicate this book to the Meyes. During his visit to Zagreb in the spring of 1977, Doug Meye suggested that I, a kid from Yugoslavia, come to study theology at Fuller Theological Seminary, in Pasadena, where he was to start his own studies that fall. His father, Robert, then Dean of Fuller and a New Testament scholar, helped make Doug's suggestion a reality. When I arrived in Pasadena in September 1977, I lived for the first few months with the Meyes, Robert and Mary and their children Marianne, Doug, and John. These were some of the happiest months of my life. Mary, affectionate and always helpful, became my U.S. mother. Marianne, also a student at Fuller at the time, was to become my colleague when I joined the faculty of Fuller in 1991. Over the course of years, she, a New Testament scholar, and I, a theologian, discussed extensively how to engage in responsible theological reading of the Scripture. To all of the Meyes, in different ways, I owe an immense debt of gratitude.